REAL ESTATE MARKETING PLAYBOOK

BRANDON DOYLE

ISBN-13: 978-1720374190

CONTENTS

INTRODUCTION

Countless marketing books have been written for real estate agents, and for a good reason: to survive in today's challenging economic climate, real estate agents must wear so many hats at once to have a chance at success, and thus need as much help as they can get.

While many real-estate marketing books offer a whole-life plan to achieving your goals or attempt to impress you with far-out tactics that may have worked for one person, one time, in a market unlike any other, this book is different. The *Real Estate Marketing Playbook* was inspired by observations and experiences over many years in the real estate business.

Concise chapters get right to the point and offer actionable advice. You'll receive a brief overview of each tactic, learn about best practices, and in most chapters, you'll hear from experts as they chime in on their struggles and successes.

This is not to say that the book is merely short; it is merely respectful of your time.

HOW TO USE THIS BOOK

Each chapter is its own contained unit. Feel free to flip to any section that intrigues you, or that addresses a situation applicable to you.

Keep in mind that it is not humanly possible to implement every idea in this book. Neither is it possible that every concept applies to every real estate agent. Just like your real estate business, every situation is unique. Use common sense to determine if a plan is right for you, your market, and your business.

This book is meant to be kept within reach throughout your business day - in the car, in your bag or briefcase, etc. It's a perfect companion when waiting for open houses to begin or for clients to arrive. It's a helpful lunchtime read to keep you in the mindset of innovation and forward movement for your business.

Anytime you need a helpful hint or a compelling idea to help boost your current or next marketing project, crack it open; even just flipping it open and reading a chapter at random could spark an idea that skyrockets your real estate business.

This book is not for those seeking a shortcut, but for those who are willing to challenge themselves to take advantage of every opportunity to grow their real estate business.

ABOUT ME

So, who am I, and why should you listen to me?

I am a second-generation real estate agent; my father Michael and I head a team serving the northwest metro of the Twin Cities in Minnesota. With decades of combined real estate experience and over 100 million dollars in completed transactions, we have a proven track record of success.

I hold a Bachelor of Science degree in Real Estate from St. Cloud State University, as well as a Master of Science in Real Estate at the University of St. Thomas. I have served on numerous association committees, been featured in many real estate magazines and blogs nationwide, and am a national real estate speaker.

All of which is to say that I offer a unique perspective on real estate marketing and am grateful for the chance to share what I know with you.

In today's uncertain market, it can be easy to get discouraged, to feel like you're not doing enough, or to get distracted by the latest marketing trend. When you feel like you're not quite sure what to do, the *Real Estate Marketing Playbook* will help you get on the right track.

As you prepare to dive in, keep in mind the wise words of Bruce Lee: "Research your own experiences for truth... Absorb what is useful... Add what is specifically your own... " He may have been talking about the intense discipline of martial arts, but the same holds true for thriving as a real estate agent.

So, let's get started.

SPHERE OF INFLUENCE

Your sphere of influence includes your family, friends, colleagues, teammates, neighbors, kids' friends' parents, former co-workers, former classmates. In short, everyone you know by name. For most of us, this totals around 200 people. Luckily for you, this is a list you've been building your entire life. The people you already know are much more likely to give you a shot than a person you've only met once or twice.

It makes sense that the relationship-based real estate industry would be intimately familiar with the value of this large circle. Having a personal connection with someone, wherein they genuinely know (at least on some level) who you are, is the best basis for establishing a professional relationship. People want to work with those they **know, like and trust,** and the more people who know, like and trust you, the better position you'll be in to grow your business.

Zvi Brand, founder, and CEO of Contactually is an expert on relationship marketing, and has this to say:

> "Relationship marketing, like most business activities, requires three key components. If you take it seriously, you'll invest in the people, processes, and systems to consistently execute on your strategy.
>
> First, relationship marketing is the act of building and maintaining 1:1 relationships with *people*. You want people to know **you**, not necessarily the corporate entity you're representing. With you on the front lines, it's critical that you possess the skills to execute on these relationship-building activities.
>
> Second, imagine if every time you got into the car, you had to figure out how to turn it on and drive?
>
> *Processes* are the recipes you build up to allow consistent and effective execution of relationship marketing tasks. Just like driving becomes a string of subconscious actions put together to get you where consciously you desire to go, relationship marketing processes are specific micro-tactics you subconsciously use."

The brand also has a unique and helpful strategy to break down relationship marketing. Take it away, Zvi:

THE CAPITAL STRATEGY OF RELATIONSHIP MARKETING

I'm going to break down relationship marketing into seven key components and give a quick summary of each...

If you want to actively engage with specific sets of people to yield specific outcomes, you need a *strategy*. And that is what we are laying out here. Each of these steps links together to help you strategize to nurture your sphere.

- Consistent execution
- Aggregate
- Prioritize
- Investigate
- Timely engagement
- Add value
- Learn and iterate

And, yes, for any of you nerds, you already noticed the mnemonic device used. What you're trying to do is build up that all-important relationship capital, and the CAPITAL system of relationship marketing is your strategy to achieve it.

CONSISTENT EXECUTION

Executing consistently is *the* most important thing to do to achieve the long-term objective. Your ability to break out of the urgent-response world (which we talked about in Chapter 3) and dedicate time to eventual outcomes will benefit you. We'll talk about how to engineer this habit.

AGGREGATE

Building and maintaining a robust database gives you a baseline to work from. Leveraging today's technology, you can create a digital representation of everyone you know – and knew.

PRIORITIZE

Not everyone will help with your goals. Who will, and how important are they? We're not going to organize the chaos of your professional sphere; we're going to prioritize who is likely to help you with your goals.

INVESTIGATE

People do business with people they know, so getting better at extracting and storing information on your prioritized relationships will give you working materials for the future.

TIMELY ENGAGEMENT

If mindshare decays, the simple solution is to have a periodic fallback pattern in case you don't connect for any reason. You'll build systems and practices for maintaining cadence, never letting mindshare slip too low.

ADD VALUE

It's not just about "following up." To make sure you're unforgettable, you want to demonstrate your value by delivering value. Guess what – sending clients a fruitcake won't cut it.

LEARN AND ITERATE

Like any marketing practice, you'll only realize the return on your investment if you track the results of your actions, iterate on what you've learned, and implement your findings.

Typically, depending on how you structure your business, between 65 and 80 percent of your income will come from your sphere of influence, so maximizing this resource is a no-brainer. There are ways to do this authentically, to nurture and grow your connections. There are also ways to *think* you are tending to your sphere that are less authentic, and therefore, less effective.

For example, many agents use automated, so-called "efficiencies," which are ways to project themselves into the minds of people in their sphere with the touch of a 'send' button. Certainly, there are effective uses of newsletters and email that add value to your relationships. However, the thoughtless overuse of email, particularly mass emails, is one of the *least* effective ways to connect with your sphere. If you're using this practice, it's a great place to start refining your approach.

Make an effort to find out what is meaningful to people in your sphere, and use that information to approach them accordingly. Some people like to chat on the phone every so often. Some need face-to-face time. You may know people for whom it's important that you contribute to, or participate in, their favorite charity event. Some people desire more hands-on attention, while some prefer less. Facebook is popular for a reason—busy people can stay connected with their friends, from the convenience of their desk chair. But, be careful how you use this tool—some in your sphere avoid Facebook, and your most insightful post would miss them entirely. Also, beware the social media time-suck—you can put in a lot of time with very little return.

The beauty of a personalized approach is that there are multiple mediums through which you can make your connections, and you can use some or all of them. Typical methods include personal phone calls, email, newsletters, in-person meetings, and social media. By incorporating a customized strategy, you will strengthen the core connection that people in your sphere have with you and remind them that you are someone they know, like and trust. This makes you the person they'll go to or send their sphere when it comes time to buy or sell a home.

CREATING AND CATEGORIZING YOUR DATABASE

By now it should be clear that clients want to work with people they know, like and trust. We've established that the people who will become part of your database are human, and as such, would like to be treated with respect. Now, let's look at how you are going to organize these contacts, friends, and leads in our ever-important database.

By its very nature, your customer database will be a list of relationships that can sustain, and ultimately grow your business (read: increasing profit, income, earnings). To that end, your database is the lifeblood of your business. There are no tools more valuable than your database, so it deserves to be created and sustained with all due respect, care, and cultivation.

Therefore, it's necessary to define and organize your database. There's a significant distinction between your database and your *mailing list*. Consider a mailing list to be a way to get leads from people who live in a shared geographic area, or from those who have signed up for more information on your website or those who attended an event you hosted, sponsored, or served as a presenter.

By contrast, your database is not just a list of names or contacts. It is a list of *relationships*. The database becomes increasingly more useful as you glean more information from these relationships through continuing to establish trust. See how it all comes full circle?

Like a mailing list, your database will have the basics including names, email addresses, websites, and phone numbers. However, your database should go beyond just the facts. Try to include birthdays, anniversaries, possibly children's birthdays, the preferred method of contact, pet information, significant hobbies or leisure pastimes. Gathering and categorizing key data points can help you to organize, and plan for marketing.

For example, entering birthdays in your database will allow you to send email greeting, make a personal call, mail a card, or even just acknowledge the birthday on social media. Similarly, knowing which of your clients are interested in your local professional sports teams allows you to create another point of contact targeting those that fall into this category. This information is valuable, and the more you carefully maintain your database, the better you can cultivate, nurture, and strengthen the bonds of the relationship, and reinforce to clients that you care about them.

The result is that you become the person that everyone in your database knows, likes and trusts. From there, you can turn prospects into customers, and profitable clients into repeat customers, and advocates for your business or service.

Categorizing your database will help you schedule your time and ensure that your time and energy address the proper issues.

Before utilizing a CRM (Customer Relationship Management) system, we maintained a physical mailing list and periodically added new names to our monthly e-newsletter drip campaign. This worked fine until we scaled up our operations and started adding a lot of additional lead sources. We found that opportunities were falling through the cracks; if someone inquired but didn't do business with us right away, we struggled to stay on top of them. Whenever we had downtime, we'd go through the notes scattered about the office, listen to old voicemails, and dig through the emails that got buried at the bottom of our inboxes. It was an inefficient way of doing business.

Putting the time into organizing our database and creating a system for follow up has had an immensely positive impact on our business. With a CRM system in place, you'll stay top of mind, and on top of your leads. In addition to helping us get organized, it allowed us to strengthen our relationships with customers and learn more about them.

SEGMENTING YOUR DATABASE

What's the good of investing in a CRM, putting in money, time and effort, if you're not going to segment and organize your network of contacts accurately? Without crucial organization, you might as well throw the whole system away and go back to spreadsheets and post-it notes. Your CRM will only work for you if you're putting the work into it.

I use Contactually as my primary resource for managing my relationships. This tool allows for 'bucketing' your relationships by how often you want to keep in touch with them. While not everyone needs to follow this system, it's an exciting way to think about organizing your contacts, which can often feel like an overwhelming and Herculean task.

When thinking about segmenting your database, you want to ask yourself two questions: *"How important is this person to my business?"* and *"How often do I want to talk to them?"* Once you've got those answered, you can categorize and segment nearly everyone in your database so that you can get to work.

However, that does not answer the question of what exactly your segmentation should look like and how you'll categorize the contacts in your network. Just knowing that a particular connection is essential to your business and that you'll want to get in touch with them isn't quite enough to build your segmentation categories. But it does give you the framework of how to think about it.

In addition to our two questions you'll need to answer, here are a few segmentation 'buckets' to try out:

* Family and friends: This is the easiest source of business for most agents, but often times they're neglected. Some agents assume that they'll automatically get this business and do not take the time to systematically follow up with their own friends and family. Only to become frustrated when they see someone they know on a Facebook post about the home they sold. Recently in addition to using Contactually, we've added First.io which allows us to identify those who are most likely to move within our database, they also have scheduling assistants available whom can set up lunch or coffee meetings for you. That way you're conveniently top of mind when a potential seller you know is most likely to list.

* Past clients: What better source for referrals than past clients? Give this segment of your database particular attention several times a year to not only maintain

such relationships but also to outreach for referrals and reviews. I recommend a monthly newsletter both physical and electronic since unfortunately, a majority of email goes unread. Automated campaigns alone are not enough though, it is essential to be making contact in person or over the phone several times throughout the year. We've had a lot of success hosting 2-3 client appreciation events each year, more on that later.

A-B-C Method: Within our sphere of influence which includes friends, family, and past clients there is a hierarchy. The most important people in your data-base are your A's, these are your raving fans and huge advocates for your business. You can rely on them for at least one transaction a year so you'll want to arm them with everything they need to spread the good word. They should be the first people you think of if you happen to have extra tickets to a sporting event, and it is certainly worth taking them out to lunch or dinner every so often. Now not everyone is as well connected or willing to help promote as your A's, it does take a specific personality type. The next subset is your B's, these people have either done business with you in the past or have provided a referral that has resulted in closed business. It is also important to stay top of mind with them and having a meaningful conversation at least once a quarter. The majority of people in your sphere of influence will fall into the category of C's, these are people whom would most likely do business with you, but you haven't had the opportunity to do business with them lately. There is no category for D's, D stands for delete. Don't waste time pursuing people who are not likely to do business with you, live out of your market area, or just don't match your personality type.

* Hot leads: These are potential customers that are pretty much ready to do business any day now and should be contacted on a very regular basis. While you may not need to keep in touch with this segment of your database on a daily basis, it's crucial to keep them up to date with any necessary information as they move through the sales process.

* Warm leads: Not quite as ready as the hot leads, this group is getting close. Consider as your warm leads those who aren't quite prepared to make the purchase yet but are showing interest. I try and keep in touch with this segment every three months to keep them warm with general updates, newsletters or check-in's in a more personal manner.

* Cold Leads: They aren't dead, but for the time being, they're cold. However, that does not mean you should ignore them altogether. Set them up on an automated drip campaign and then check in periodically. Watch for increased activity such as opening your newsletters, clicking on links, viewing more homes on your website, or an elevated seller score if you're using a service such as First.io

* Referral Partners: Local business people, other real estate agents and any other partners that you give referrals to and vice versa. Referrals are the lifeblood of the real estate business and maintaining a relationship for this segment is crucial to your success.

* Catchall: Come across someone who doesn't quite fit into any of the categories, but who should not be removed from your database entirely? You'll want to place them here.

This methodology is not a one-size-fits-all segmentation outline; part of building a database is making it personal for you. Without that personalization, you are less likely to make use of your database or CRM system, rendering it useless.

The most important thing to remember as you're working through the segmentation process of your database is that nothing is set in stone. The best segmentation is one that is always in flux because you are keeping it up to date with your business. Once your hot leads make it through your pipeline and have happily settled in their new home, it's time to move them to your past client's segment and ask them for a referral or online review.

Allowing for flexibility in your database segmentation will strengthen your database overall as you build it out to optimize your business.

RESOURCES

http://www.contactually.com
http://www.first.io
http://www.limelightmarketingsystems.com

CLIENT APPRECIATION EVENTS

Inviting clients to client appreciation parties is an excellent opportunity to call your past clients and update their information in your CRM. We utilize tools such as Eventbrite for registration which also us to ask for contact information we may be missing. Everyone likes getting invited to a party, so it is a great excuse to call and catch up. The invitations and event reminders will keep you top of mind regardless of whether they're able to attend or not. Remember it is the thought that counts.

Demonstrating your gratitude towards past and present clientele has the potential to increase your referrals, expand your database, and have valuable face-to-face time with your business's bread and butter: people. Below are some tips to help you craft the perfect client appreciation bash.

EXPAND YOUR GUEST LIST.

Don't stop at inviting former clients to your client appreciation bash. Instead, expand your network and ask neighbors, local businesses, friends, family, associates, and the like to attend. Doing so creates a coveted in-person opportunity to build relationships and broaden your reach.

THINK BIG AND EXPLORE SPONSORS

You don't want to blow your budget with a client appreciation event, so consider enlisting local businesses and associates as sponsors of the big day. Consider partnering with your preferred lender, home warranty company, handyman, general contractor, or any other service provider which your clients may need. Not only does enlisting sponsors soften the financial blow of throwing an impressive party, but it also connects you to other entrepreneurs, widening your database and sources for leads.

USE LOCAL EVENTS OR HOLIDAYS AS A MEDIUM

Whether the local high school football team just won the big game, or a significant holiday is just around the corner, piggybacking client appreciation events with established happenings is a natural tie-in that can also boost your attendance. One popular idea is conducting a pie giveaway during the Thanksgiving holiday season or hosting a Super Bowl viewing party. Both approaches create a natural theme and an opportunity for camaraderie between hosts and attendees.

MAKE IT PERSONAL

Invitations for client appreciation events shouldn't be one-size-fits-all. While time management demands some efficiency in regards to your invites, consider sending handwritten notes clients you remember well, or for associates with whom you have an upcoming meeting. Perhaps you're sending an invite to someone who lives on the same street as a listing you just began to publicize—this is a natural opportunity to make a personal connection that could benefit your business *and* lead to more confirmed RSVPs.

Cultivating leads and relationships is equally as important as the active work of helping clients buy or sell a home. Securing the future health of your business depends on what you do in the present and showing clients that you're a business who cares is an excellent start.

LOCATION, LOCATION, LOCATION

Choose a place based on who your average client is. If you are a luxury listing agent, consider asking one of your clients with a million-dollar listing if you can host the party in their house as a way to advertise their home. If you work with a lot of families with small children, you could host an event at an apple orchard, local park, or rent out a movie theater. The more memorable the client appreciation party, the more top of mind you will remain when it comes time for clients, or their friends, to buy or sell their home.

TAKE PHOTOS

It is essential to capture lots of photos and videos at the event to post on social media, be sure to tag your clients and ask them to share on their own page. Whether you hire a photographer or take them yourself just don't forget this important step. After the event, you can send them out to attendees along with a thank you that will remind them of the fun they had and keep you top of mind.

Don't forget clients after you get that commission check. A client appreciation party is a fun, unique way to stay top of mind with your real estate clients. The opportunities are endless and are limited only by your imagination and your budget. Don't ignore this valuable opportunity to stay connected with clients, lay the groundwork for future clients, and to ensure the future health of your business.

RESOURCES

http://realtormag.realtor.org/tool-kit/follow-up/article/great-customer-appreciation-events-for-every-season
http://travisrobertson.com/blog/repeat-referral-client/

EMAIL MARKETING

The modern tech user is accustomed to sifting through junk mail and only spends time on communication that matters. That's why crafting an e-newsletter with a high open rate is so important. A compelling headline and engaging content go a long way in cultivating a professional connection.

What's more, refining your e-mail marketing efforts don't have to be complicated. Effective communication via newsletter takes only a few simple tweaks and mindful adjustments to get the most out appearing in a potential client's inbox. Below are some ideas on how to add value to your newsletter and garner those coveted open rates that will let you know you're on the right track.

CREATE STIRRING BUT HONEST SUBJECT LINES

Titles and subject lines aren't just formalities. They're the best chance to grab your reader's attention. So, how exactly can you make your subject line pop? For starters, be clear. It's tempting to favor intrigue in a subject line (and that's not a bad instinct, either!) but you're better off being straightforward about what your newsletter will discuss. Cliché subject lines won't grab attention, and those that create a big show of mystery will only work once.

Avoid generic subject lines like: "Our Monthly Newsletter"; instead try engaging with emotions and asking questions. You might also try to make your FROM LINE YOUR FIRST NAME INSTEAD OF YOUR BUSINESS'S—IT CREATES A PERSON-TO-PERSON CONNECTION.

ALSO, KEEP IN MIND THAT SHORT AND SWEET PLAYS BEST. AIM FOR ABOUT FIFTY CHARACTERS, AND FRONT END THE MOST CRUCIAL INFORMATION IN YOUR SUBJECT LINE—THAT WAY YOU WON'T LOSE IMPACT BY E-MAIL ALERTS THAT CUT-OFF LENGTHY SUBJECT LINES. OTHER PROVEN APPROACHES INCLUDE:

- **Personalize:** Use your client's name in the subject line, especially at the beginning of a question.
- **Wordplay:** Making a pun, or referencing a relevant song lyric or iconic quote can be a light way of creating familiarity and intrigue.
- **By the Numbers:** A subject line that's informative—using a relevant and surprising statistic for instance—can pique their interest
- **So Emotional:** Play towards emotions in your subject line. Hopes? Fears? A happy occasion?

Keep it human, and it'll be easier to forge a connection.

- **Get a Sense of What's Working and What's Not** Avoid spinning your wheels and wondering why one newsletter generated more open rates while the following month's generated less with A/B testing.

Numerous content management programs can help you track and compare your newsletter open rates month-to-month. This kind of data is invaluable in fine-tuning your approach to newsletters and subject lines and can help you replicate success or adjust your methods appropriately. A bonus tip: if a client hasn't engaged with your newsletter in quite a while, why not bring it up in a subject line? It doesn't hurt to check in on missed connections, and it may inspire more engagement.

WHAT'S ON THE INSIDE COUNTS, TOO

If your main priority is bolstering your open rates, you might not think that what's *inside* your newsletter can make a compelling initial impact. However, many inboxes and smartphone e-mail alerts offer a preview of e-mail content—usually an e-mail's first line. Pay close attention to the opening sentence of your newsletter, and you might just double your open rates.

Think of the first line of your newsletter as a sub-header, an opportunity to meaningfully expand on your subject line and boost those coveted open rates. Try addressing your client by their name in the first line, then get right to the point. With the subject line out of the way, you should use the body's first line to dive into the meat of what you mean to say.

As you fine-tune your newsletter practices and draw a broader audience for your business's messages, keep these behind-the-scenes tips in mind, and you'll earn the visibility your newsletters have been craving.

Resources

http://www.limelightmarketingsystems.com
http://www.mailchimp.com
http://www.contactually.com
https://www.curaytor.com/
blog/12-Email-Marketing-Stats-to-Live-By/

AGENT REFERRALS

One of the benefits of being a licensed real estate agent is the ability to legally collect a fee for referring clients to other agents. This, of course, goes both ways, agents who have built up a referral network are able to earn additional revenue by sending and receiving referrals. The best way to become the agent that gets the referrals in your area is to build relationships by networking with agents in markets that typically move to your area. For example, an agent that does business in the gulf coast of Florida or Arizona may want to network with agents from Minnesota, a lot of retirees are 'snowbirds' and own property down south that they stay at during the winter months.

When it comes to Agent to Agent referrals, this sometimes is a popularity contest, and brand loyalty may come into play. This is the reason why I believe in building relationships. Whether it's within NAR, your State Association, or within your company, relationships will always be the key. Wouldn't you rather have other agents raving about you, so you don't have to sell yourself?

Last year I received at least 10 referrals from different agents. It is also important that when they check you up on social media, your profile has personality and is very inviting.
– Joseph Magsaysay

National conferences are a great place to meet agents for potential referrals, however, don't be "That guy" that just collects business cards, a handful of solid relationships are better than a hundred acquittances. While we're at it, don't add everyone to your generic email newsletter, that is called spam, and we're all getting enough of that already.

If you aren't able to make it to events, you can still build relationships with agents in other markets by contributing to Facebook groups. By continuing to share your knowledge and provide value to other members of the group you'll gain their trust. Then when the time comes when someone has a referral for your area, you'll find that other members are tagging you before you even see the request. Having five different people say you're a recommended agent for your area looks a heck of a lot better then you replying to promote yourself.

If you're with one of the major real estate brands, likely you'll have a referral network in place, be sure to fill out your profile completely so that you have best chance to be selected. Even if you're with a smaller company, many agents will simply search online to find the best fit for their referral regardless of brand. If I don't already know an agent in a particular market that I have a referral for, I tend to look at reviews on Zillow, productivity and average price point on Homesnap to determine if it's a good fit. Agents search for potential referral candidates the same way consumers do, the agent with the best online presence will typically get more opportunities. This past year we've had three agents refer us business that simply found us online.

Referrals aren't necessarily always out of market either, sometimes if an agent is too busy or has chosen to specialize in a certain niche, they may share opportunities with other agents they trust. For example, an agent may have a lot of listings that generate buyer leads but doesn't have time to work with them. They can send these out to hungry agents in exchange for a referral fee upon closing. Look for agents in your company that handle REO properties or work exclusively with a builder. Start by offering to host open houses for them, once you've built rapport ask if they have any sign calls or leads that need to be followed up with.

There are also companies that specialize in facilitating agent to agent referrals, they typically collect an additional referral fee on each transaction, and there may be an up-front cost to join.

Referral Exchange promises to match your outgoing referral with 3 great agents and will pay up to a 25% referral fee. Paid members have the opportunity to receive referrals from other agents that have been qualified as well as leads from their site topagentsranked.com

HomeLight has gained a lot of traction recently since launching a consumer-focused advertising campaign.

The premise is that consumers are matched with agents that specialize in their area and price point, the recommendations are based on the agent's previous transaction history. They essentially charge 25% to act as a middleman for the agents who are willing to pay it. I was very disappointed when I followed up with a seller lead only to find out she had decided to go with the agent that HomeLight recommended, I guess that just proves that it does work.

Agent Pronto is a hybrid between the two, it matches consumers with an agent in their area based on experience but also allows agents to input outgoing referrals. When working with any of these sites be sure to fill out your profile completely and respond promptly to any inquiries as you'll be competing against two other agents every time. Any outgoing referrals you submit should have given you permission to do so. Otherwise, it may be an invasion of their privacy. Remember when they signed up on your website they did not give you permission to resell or share their contact information.

RESOURCES

Facebook Groups
www.referralexchange.com
www.homelight.com
www.agentpronto.com

NETWORK REFERRALS

Networking is a broad term, it could refer to attending events, being an active member of a group, or just generally following up and making connections. Real estate agents are natural networkers, our clients rely on us for referrals for everything from carpet cleaning to a mortgage lender. Molly McKinley, VP of Marketing at First.io describes this as relationship marketing which has evolved and becomes intertwined with all other aspects of the marketing wheel. Essentially, relationship marketing turns agents and brokers into sought-out local influencers.

How often do your neighbors and friends call you to ask about finding a painter, plumber, roofer or interior designer? Probably a lot. And if it is something that annoys you, think again.

You want to be perceived as valuable, as someone to call for advice -- or in a crisis. If you are regularly helping people, when you ask them for help (or to consider using you for a listing) it isn't a sales pitch. The value is not just between you and potential listers. It is also between you and those that might refer work (like tradespeople). Consider using the 3/1 rule. Consider helping three times, before asking for anything in return. It's a good practice in business -- and life!

In addition to having a list of trusted vendors, be sure to also develop relationships with those whom would naturally be talking to people when may have a desire to move. Financial planners, wedding planners, tax accountants, divorce attorneys, probate attorneys, and builder representatives are all great sources of referrals. There are groups such as BNI that are dedicated to facilitating an environment for referrals to be exchanged. If you visit the BNI website and look up your local area, I'm sure you'll find a top producer has already established themselves with a successful group. The real estate agent spot typically doesn't stay vacant for long and starting a group of your own can be challenging. I remember emailing, calling, and sending letters to local business owners to invite them to our weekly meetings, eventually, we got to 12 members, but then it all fell apart. Don't underestimate the time requirement, weekly networking groups can be a great source of business but aren't for everyone. Nothing is stopping you from meeting new people and building relationships on your own.

Building your network doesn't happen overnight. It is a long-term process that takes effort and dedication. It is the antithesis of buying leads, cold calling FSBOs, and other techniques that aren't related to building a relationship. It takes effort. But it can also be fun.

There is another aspect to relationship marketing. It involves learning to listen. Instead of inviting someone for coffee and going on about the latest trends in kitchen remodels, or the hotness of a particular neighborhood's sales, go to coffee and listen. You might hear something that will give you an idea of how to be helpful, or for content you could put on your website. The opportunity arises in conversation, and we all yearn to simply be heard. If you open your mind, pay attention and release expectations of transacting with each meeting, you will create depth and integrity in your relationships. And, it's personally rewarding to nurture your network in this way. The business will follow when you show up with genuine care.

This type of marketing is not at all like creating a clickbait blog post. Relationship marketing is about getting to know people -- and serving them. If you remember the golden rule and treat others the way you would want to be treated with every interaction, you are well on your way to mastering the art of this practice.

RESOURCES

https://www.meetup.com/topics/professional-networking/
https://www.bni.com/
https://www.networkafterwork.com/

RELOCATION

Relocation service companies rely on real estate companies and their agents to assist their high powered corporate clients in moving valuable employees. While this can sometimes mean high commissions and valuable networking experience, these do not come without a price.

While most relocation referrals are handled through a relocation company, it sometimes happens that a client will prefer to work with you instead of through the recommended real estate company or agent. Before you take that listing or work with a buyer consider that relocation companies are notorious for their fees, and also check first with the transferee's relocation company to make sure you are allowed to represent the transferee. Not all companies allow this, and a transferee could lose their benefits.

Expect to pay high referral fees to these companies, even if a client requests you. As recently as 2016, referral fees through Cartus, one of the nation's largest corporate relocation services, rose from 37.5% to 40%. Agents outside the relocation company's network faced fees up to 42%. This number is only expected to rise among all national relocation companies. The bottom line is that third-parties like these make more in referral fees than the agents themselves.

Additionally, it's easy to get overwhelmed when working with relocating clients, because of the human factor and time constraints. Relocation clients are not your typical buyers or sellers. Relocating is right up there on the top items that are most stressful in one's life. You need to be able to empathize with their situation which is usually dictated by their employers. Also, you may be the only face to face contact a transferee has through their entire relocation process and will depend upon you for extensive information, and if they are buyers, expect you devote your entire time with them while they are looking for a home. This can be very stressful as the transferee may only have one to three days to see houses, depending on what their company allows for in the home buying process. Communication is key! A smooth transition means a happy family, which equates to a productive employee for the employer, and a satisfied relocation company for future referrals.

Depending on your real estate company's structure and process, you may also be answering to your company and/or directly with the relocation company. Working with transferees requires updating the relocation company regularly, and you will, again, be expected to provide extensive information materials, and to provide regular updates, as relocation company's answer not only to their corporate client but also the transferees. Between this kind of micromanaging and working extra hard, it's easy to see why many agents can burn out working in relo.

However, for all the hard, extra effort to working in relocation, it is still a great way to get high-value referral opportunities and experience. Price points tend to be higher, as workers whose companies go to all the trouble of relocating tend to be higher income, all of which could add up to more commission for you.

Working in relocation can also help you break into a higher-end market via referrals, which you can then use to get more business and even more references outside of the relocation company networks. Transferees appreciate how hard you work for them and refer you to their sphere of influence. Last but not least, relocation can get you tons of practice and experience, which will come in handy for the rest of your career.

Check out SIRVA, Crown World Mobility and Cartus for more information on working with relocation companies each have their own specialty and offerings. For example, SIRVA assists international moves, and offers clients not only real estate help but also help with immigration and Visa issues as well.

Other things to keep in mind regarding relocation include the fact that these relocation companies are highly susceptible to economic factors; for example, shortly after the Great Recession in 2008, the national behemoths declared protective bankruptcy, and agent fees became scarce. Currently, while the real estate market continues to improve, companies that are willing to relocate workers aren't doing so as much these days.

Furthermore, domestically, corporate relocation tends to be limited to major metropolitan areas; while foreign corporate growth in regions like China and Europe has a brighter outlook than it does for the majority of the United States. So, while relocation is still a viable method for success for real estate agents, approach it with guarded optimism.

Visit Worldwide ERC.org for the latest in relocation including, trends, products and services, worldwide statistics and becoming a CRP (Certified Relocation Professional).

RESOURCES

SIRVA
Crown World Mobility
Cartus
WorldWideERC.org

PAID LEAD SOURCES

One way to generate leads online is to purchase ads on third-party real estate websites, such as Zillow/Trulia, Homes.com, or Realtor. com. Most of these sites require you to pay for the opportunity to be one of up to three agents posted on the page being viewed by potential homebuyers, who are beginning their search via these sites. Searches and ads appear based on zip codes.

One thing to keep in mind when planning a strategy around these ads is that people who peruse these sites will be at different levels of readiness to become actual buyers. Some people like to look at for-sale houses just for fun. Some might be looking for valuation information for the sale of their own home. Some might be looking seriously, but still be six months to a year from buying. Some might be interested but lack the financial ability to buy. And, of course, some will be ready to pull the trigger right away. You'll encounter all of these people. Some will be interested in talking to you, and some won't.

According to Zillow, only 1.9% of their visitors are serious shoppers. They also indicated that 37.9% were double counted, and 19.9% were looking at rentals. The remaining 40.3% were described as voyeurs

The typical online lead is a potential buyer who is about six months from an actual purchase. This can present an opportunity, in that if you connect with people at this point, you can be the one they have in mind as they get more serious in their process. This type of lead will require much more follow up and education to woo the buyers, and it can be time-intensive to convert leads like this. It can take eight to ten follow-up contacts before someone decides to work with you.

I've also had the experience of making eight to ten contacts with someone and had them *not* sign with me, either because they go with someone else, or because they don't buy at all.

An immediate response is also critical to making an impression with these leads. Generally, a potential win goes to the agent who reaches the customer first. For this, I highly recommend checking out CallAction (www.callaction.co)

Usually, sites like Realtor.com will require an annual contract that you cannot get out of early. Recently Zillow has moved to a month to month model. However, they will offer you additional benefits if you're willing to sign a 6-month contract. Realtor.com offers both exclusive and non-exclusive leads with a min. Guarantee each month. Previously Zillow's pricing was based on a guaranteed number of impressions, but they've since switched to a "Share of Voice" structure which has increased transparency allowing you to see what percentage of the overall advertising you and each of your competitors are getting. They also provide a tool that allows you to estimate the number of leads, cost per lead, and projected return on investment. Zip code prices will vary by region and tend to run around $2,000 per month. This cost may be more manageable for larger teams and already-productive agents to absorb, who have the resources to buy entire territories and capture as many leads as possible. I recommend committing to at least a 50% share of voice and staying within the top 3 advertisers in your area to get the best results. As of the time of this writing Zillow Group has changed the way leads are delivered, they're now calling the leads themselves and doing warm live transfers to the next available agent on the list. While the amount of leads we're receiving has gone down substantially, the quality of the ones we're connecting with has certainly increased. It is too early to tell how this new method of delivery will play out but it is something worth keeping an eye on. I do commend Zillow Group for taking the time to understand what their visitors are looking for and make an attempt to provide a superior customer experience.

Compared to the pay-per-click website leads, 3rd party portal leads tend to convert at a higher rate, and more quickly. This is because they're typically inquiring on a property they're interested as opposed being forced to register to see pictures or property information as is the case with PPC website leads. Because of this online portal leads tend to be more expensive, currently in our market we're seeing an average of $100 for a Zillow lead which has been converting between 4-6% in about 2 months whereas our PPC leads are only costing us around $15 each but are converting around 1-2% after 6-12 months.

RESOURCES

www.zillow.com

www.realtor.com

www.homes.com

www.callaction.co

GETTING FOUND ONLINE

I magine that you are about to give a presentation to a stadium full of people who are looking to buy or sell a home. My guess is you'd show up prepared and looking your best, with up-to-date information and helpful ideas. To the thousands of people searching the Internet for information on neighborhoods, properties, and agents, your online presence is your first impression and your best chance to impress.

Does your website drive traffic, present your business well, and help you sell? Just as you continue to hone your sales and presentation skills, it's vital to continue to evolve your website and social media presence to grow your business and increase your reach, and, ultimately, your sales. Here are some ideas to take your online presence to the next level.

LEVERAGE PORTALS

Make sure your profile on your webpage is complete and up-to-date. Aggregate enough reviews to be on page one of search engine results within your community and ensure all your past sales are showing up. Having lots of citations which all display the same, accurate info about your business helps to improve your ranking in local search results. Other sites to leverage include Facebook, Google, and your broker's website. You can use a local citation tool like MozLocal, Yext, or BrightLocal to find other directories and third-party websites you can add your listing.

GET LOCAL

Capitalize on the opportunity that comes with hyper-local content and long tail keywords. Use your online content to become THE local agent. When your target audience is searching your neighborhood or area of expertise, you want to be the first listing to show up that isn't a brokerage or third-party website.

You can achieve that by demonstrating your knowledge of your region with content about community features, businesses, and events. In an ideal world, you would add a new piece of local content each week. Then share your articles with larger websites and include backlinks to yours. You could also ask local businesses to share the articles you write about them on their site.

MAKE IT MOBILE

Think through how your clients are finding and experiencing your website. Mobile digital media time in the US is now at 51% compared to desktop usage (42%), meaning that people are most likely viewing your site on a mobile device like a smartphone, so make sure your website is responsive and works when displayed on a phone or mobile device.

ADD VIDEO

When used correctly, video can be a powerful form of content that adds value for your visitors and makes a significant contribution to your SEO strategy. Make sure to have a clear goal for what you want to communicate with your video and keep it short, entertaining, and easy to watch.

ALLOW FOR INTERACTIVITY

At a minimum, your website should include your contact information, home search, and some information about you, your company, and the local area. I also recommend having testimonial pages, and some buyer and seller resources. To add another layer of value and drive interactivity, consider incorporating different ways for visitors to interact with your site.

Three frequent calls to action are "Search," "What's my Home Worth?" and "How's the Market?" Allow visitors to search by community, neighborhood, schools, price point, open houses, new construction, luxury, waterfront, or foreclosures, depending on your market. Lifestyle searches are cool new way agents in some markets are capturing more buyers. Ready Chat is a great tool to engage people while they're on your website. Also, make sure you utilize social sharing buttons and include links so visitors can follow you.

Make sure you're regularly reviewing your website's metrics to see where your traffic is coming from, what people are doing on your site, and where they go next. Your website has the potential to enhance your brand, deliver leads, and help you close more business. Consider investing some additional time and effort to ensure you're making the most of the real estate you have online.

It is essential for your website to be a reflection of who you are and the services you offer. Consider your website your central business hub to which all of your marketing should flow; it is where consumers will go to learn more about you and your company, search for homes, and read testimonials.

You want to stand out from your competition, and that means not having the same website like every other agent at your brokerage. If you must use the website provided by your brokerage, at least customize the pages to reflect your style and personality.

Purchasing a domain name is a simple, cost-effective way for consumers to be able to find you more quickly. If you think that the average person will type in yourbrokersname.com/yourname, you're wrong. Consumers likely are not conscious of the broker relationship, or of the significance of connecting to your specific website, and they will just go to your broker's site. Having a web domain consistent with your name, brand or local area will help consumers find you.

Since it is *your* website, you should build and host it yourself, or hire someone to do this for you. Make sure you own the content and are the sole beneficiary of all of your hard work. You don't want to build on the rented land, and you don't want to build up someone else's SEO, only to have them take it when you either switch brokerages or stop paying for that service.

There are many real estate website companies that offer a full range of services. Picking the right one depends on your budget, technological savvy, and goals. Think about what you need, and how much time you're willing to invest before you make a decision.

I personally spend about 10 hours a week maintaining our team's website and creating new original content, including blog posts. A consistent flow of new material keeps viewers engaged and coming back to revisit the site. It also keeps the website fresh in the eyes of search engines, as I'm always adjusting content to match popular search terms.

At a bare minimum, your website should have information about you, and a way for the consumer to contact you. You may also want to have a testimonial page that highlights real reviews from your past clients. Most real estate websites include a way to look at local listings, either through an IDX provider or via a link to their broker's home search function.

Real estate is local, and your website is an excellent place for you to demonstrate your knowledge of the local market. If you're adept at writing, blogs are a great way to engage your audience and talk about what is going on in your community.

THE IMPORTANCE OF SOCIAL PROOF: REVIEWS AND TESTIMONIALS

Online ratings, reviews, and testimonials—known collectively as social proof—are some of the most critical tools in a small business owner's arsenal. After all, most of us turn to the internet for guidance before trying a new restaurant, seeing a movie, or buying a product. The same is true for enlisting the services of a business. Reviews and testimonials make an emotional appeal to consumers while providing first-hand insight into a business's ability to deliver. Consider a few pieces of the rationale below to understand the value of social proof, and why its inclusion on your website can make all the difference when fielding new business.

SOCIAL PROOF BOLSTERS YOUR IDENTITY

For those who have come across your business online but do not yet know you, reviews and testimonials act as a firsthand account of who you are as a service provider. Because reviews and testimonials are cited to specific people, sometimes with their e-mails or social media handles attached, there's a personal component at play. Potential customers trust reviews and testimonials more when they can believe that the information is genuine, which is just one reason why positive reviews and testimonials can be so powerful.

SOCIAL PROOF SEPARATES YOU FROM THE COMPETITION

Let's say you're a real estate agent operating in an area with dozens of other professionals. While your qualifications and area specialties may be similar to your cohorts', you can set yourself apart by highlighting personal reviews and testimonials that speak to your character, personality, and working style.

Imagine you're a customer, faced with two agents with near identical experience and credentials; only one of those agents has glowing testimonials recounting positive experiences and lasting connections made with clients. Wouldn't you be more inclined to work with the agent who has a proven track record of success with his or her clientele?

Now that the importance of social proof has been made clear, you might be wondering how to go about collecting reviews and testimonials from former clients.

For starters, keep in mind that reviews and testimonials don't have to be lengthy or long-winded. A straightforward sentence or two about a positive personal experience with your business can go a long way. At the close of a transaction, consider providing a comment card with room for clients to write a few reflections. You can also touch base via e-mail and ask politely for a review of their experience working with you.

If you have regular and repeat clientele, these are excellent candidates for reviews and referrals, as they'll know your business well and will likely be happy to contribute their perspective. If you're unsure about asking for reviews and testimonials, you could always incentivize this process in a small way. For instance, you may offer a slight discount in exchange for the feedback you could later use online.

Whichever way you gather social proof of your business's positive performance, there's no question that public reviews and testimonials are invaluable in drawing new clientele and bolstering your online presence. If you want to stand out and inspire interest, there's no better way than to have past clients vouch for your work.

RESOURCES

Business.google.com

Facebook.com/pages

Moz.com/local

Yext

BrightLocal

Yelp.com

Domains: GoDaddy.com

Broker Websites: TRIBUS

Team Websites: Firepoint, Commissions Inc, Boomtown

Full Custom Team/Individual Websites: Cuyrator, Real Estate Webmasters

Individual Template Websites: Chime, Agent Image, TorchX

ONLINE PROFILES: SOCIAL MEDIA

You are likely already familiar with what social media is, how it works, and how inescapable it is, so we won't go into too much detail in this chapter about those aspects of social media. However, what we will say is that there are a few keys to success in using social media for your real estate business. They are:

BE WHERE YOUR MARKET IS!

Be on the platforms that your market uses; if your target market is young, affluent families, they are likely active on Instagram. Don't waste your time, energy and advertising dollars on your Pinterest page or promoted posts on Twitter if your ideal client isn't using those platforms.

USE PLATFORMS ORGANICALLY

Focus on using your social media to do three things:

1. Start a conversation – don't go straight for the sale; ask genuine questions and provide helpful information.
2. Add value by way of engaging or helpful content – share interesting articles, answer questions; prove that you are there to help.
3. Promote your business, as well as the business of other realtors – social media relationships, like real-world relationships, are an exchange of give and get.

The truth of the matter when it comes to social media is that at best, it may be helpful in finding leads, but it will not garner you a sale on its own.

Avoid promoted posts or leaning too heavily into paid ads; users of social media are wising up to companies that use social media to sell all the time and tend to ignore all but the most viral posts.

Also, resist the temptation to buy followers or friends; while it may have been true in the early days of social media that the number of followers meant success, that is no longer. Grow your base organically by doing searches and contacting friends and clients before requesting to add them to your list.

Lastly, because algorithms can and do change without warning or concern to how it might affect people, your brilliant ad campaign might amount to nothing. It is not under your control, so investing too heavily into advertising on places like Facebook might ultimately backfire on you.

REMEMBER: IT'S ALL ABOUT PERCEPTION

Use your social media channels to promote your brand and provide essential business information on your profiles, the way you want others to perceive you. Choose your content carefully!

MEASURE YOUR METRICS

There are many tools on each platform that will tell you how audiences are interacting with your content. Keep track of what gains interest to indicate how you're doing, and to guide you as you plan campaigns and posts.

SOCIAL MEDIA PLANNING AND STRATEGY PER PLATFORM

Social media should not be a standalone plan or after-thought in your real estate marketing strategy. For each platform, use lots of videos and photos whenever possible.

FACEBOOK

You can easily build a free business profile that will allow you to run ads. However, a word of caution:

according to Facebook, in 2016, 64% of all business pages were set up incorrectly, and close to 28,000 business pages are deleted per year as a result.

Use your photo galleries to host a rotation of albums for current listings and events but update them immediately; nothing gives a worse impression of a business page than an out-of-date, neglected profile. Invite people to your events and open houses, and always respond to questions and comments on your page promptly.

Facebook users can engage with your content in several ways: they can like it, share it, click on links, and comment. Posts with photos and videos get 80% more engagement than posts that are plain text.

Joseph Magsaysay Team Leader of Impact Team at Keller Williams Realty in Chesterfield, MO has this to say about Facebook:

The beauty of Facebook is that you can easily engage your audience (family, friends, customers, clients, and fellow REALTORS) through very catchy or powerful Facebook posts. Yes, having a Facebook Business Page is important for business owners, but it's still very important though to still be engaged on your personal page. When it comes to Social Media, authenticity is the key. Social Media is the collective of online communication channels dedicated to community-based input, interaction, content-sharing and collaboration. The audience can easily see when someone is authentic.

In my case, all of my friends know I am a REALTOR. They also know that am a Foodie. They know that I love food and adore food. They know that I love traveling as well. One common mistake of REALTORS is that they try to engage on Facebook by just sharing a listing or advertisement from their business pages without even describing what that "share" is all about. One must master the art of posting. Some say that you should only post on Facebook 4 times a day, maximum! I respectfully disagree. I love being in the moment. I love posting the important things that I think need to be shared. For example:

1. My son, Geno, ate 10 chicken nuggets at Chick-Fil-A. He looked so cute, so I decided to snap a photo of him. Two hours later I saw a very unique home and posted about it. So that is already 2 posts in the last 2 hours.

2. I had a fun closing, and my client wrote a review on my business page. I then shared this review on my personal page.

Bottom line is, live in the moment. Be current. Do not post something special the following day when this something special is occurring right now.

The examples mentioned above proves that it is hard to limit your posts to a maximum of 4 a day. There is just no way especially if you are really "social."

Don't get caught up in vanity metrics that don't matter, remember you can't bring 'Likes' to the bank and cash them. Like Joseph said, it's all about authenticity and engagement. We'll cover paid Facebook advertising in a separate chapter.

LINKEDIN

Linkedin is helpful if you work with corporate clients or in commercial real estate.

Build yourself a Company Page and take advantage of the advanced graphics and layout capabilities.

Use the Advanced Search tool to find local contacts. As you would with your Facebook page, post lots of interesting material, and offer to answer questions whenever you can. On your Business Profile Page, you also have access to LinkedIn's analytics tools to help you segment and target your audience and reach new audiences through ads. The most important feature on LinkedIn is The Sales Navigator tool.

The tool helps with audience targeting and lead generation. Features of the tool include Real-time sales updates, including insights on your accounts and leads, as well as potential new leads.

LinkedIn users can engage with your content in several ways: they can like, comment, and share posts, they can endorse and recommend your company and skills, and they can sign up to follow your business page to receive news and information.

Users on LinkedIn value, and are looking for, professionally relevant content, which means your message will be more engaged with when it conveys expertise in your niche field.

LinkedIn also has professional groups options, where you can join industry-related groups. You can join up to 50 groups per individual account. Maximize the opportunity to use these groups to expand your audience and generate referrals and leads.

TWITTER

It's easy to get buried on Twitter, so while you should consider this platform if your target market tends to use it, don't rely on it too much to get you leads. As with other social media, avoid getting involved in controversial discussions, use high-quality photos and videos whenever possible, and share local content, not only about listings but news, events, and announcements.

Include a link to your business page in your bio and use a current headshot for your avatar. Take advantage of all the tools on the platform to help you find people to follow. Use hashtags thoughtfully; only apply them when your tweet is relevant to the topic at hand.

INSTAGRAM

Unlike most other social media platforms, Instagram is actually on the rise as of 2018. Its users engage almost ten times more than users do on Facebook, and it is primed for SEO via hashtags and geolocation.

Instagram can be helpful in getting leads when your past clients follow you; by posting regularly and tagging people in photos, you stay top of mind when followers want to refer their friends or family to a reputable agent. Simple editing tools also allow you to post beautiful photos of listings or events.

Furthermore, Instagram Stories are like the press kit of tomorrow; these posts disappear after 24 hours and are perfect for time-sensitive events. Also, Business Profiles give you tons of data, including traffic, clicks, and demographics. Adding keywords to your profile name and bio will gather you even more data.

SOCIAL MEDIA MANAGEMENT TOOLS

While each platform has tools to help you manage your engagement, there are many quality third-party tools as well. Hootsuite, HubSpot, Tweetdeck, Buffer, and SproutSocial can be used to promote your content across multiple platforms from one publishing place, saving you time and making your marketing more effective.

A useful tool will have a robust scheduling tool, a link condenser, the ability to customize posts per platform, and have analytics and provide statistics for your published content. A good tool will also allow you to use it as a listening platform to track and monitor your competition as well.

The downsides of using automation tools are that you may become too reliant on it to push out content that you fail to monitor your channels daily to respond to questions, complaints, or customer requests. You also run the risk of not customizing your content enough for each platform. If customers just see the same content across different platforms, they can be turned off. They assume it is just a machine pushing it out, rather than a responsive human.

BEST PRACTICES FOR CONTENT CREATION

Across all platforms, when determining what to post, it's good to remember that your content should accomplish one or more of the following objectives:

Offer Advice - Social media platforms allow you the opportunity to provide useful advice to your audience while simultaneously reinforcing your status as an expert in your field. Inform your audience of things they don't know, weigh in on topical issues in your area, and provide suggestions.

Educate Others - Social media provides an excellent opportunity to educate your audience about your business and industry. Take advantage of this opportunity to showcase your knowledge by sharing little-known information to your audience.

Entertain Your Followers - Share funny videos, photos, or goofy memes to help create a bond between you and your followers. However, stay away from controversial topics, issues, politics and so on, or you'll risk alienating some of your followers.

Engage with Your Audience - ask your followers' advice on anything from what accessory you should wear to your next open house, to which new headshot they prefer. Posts that invite your followers to engage with you can help pave the way from follower to customer.

Giveaways & Contests - People love giveaways. Gift cards to local restaurants, retailers, or destinations, can be used to turn your social media posts into a fun giveaway and will almost always boost audience engagement.

RESOURCES

www.facebook.com

www.linkedin.com

www.twitter.com

www.instagram.com

www.Hootsuite.com

www.HubSpot.com

www.Tweetdeck.com

www.Buffer.com

www.SproutSocial.com

PAID WEBSITE TRAFFIC

Once you've experimented with generating organic web traffic, you may be ready for the next step: websites designed solely to generate leads, which are funded by pay-per-click ads. Examples of these include Firepoint, Commissions Inc., and Boomtown.

These sites are basically 'shovel-ready.' They are set up for you, branded with your information, and licensed to you. The service is contract-based and more expensive than purchased ads. But in some cases, they can guarantee the number of leads you will get. You'll need to have a substantial budget to commit to this approach. Costs may start at about $500 per month, but most effective lead generation website budgets are closer to $2,000 per month.

Lead generation sites used to be the best method to get leads because these companies are adept at directing traffic to agents. However, as more companies have jumped into the fray, there are now so many similar websites that it's hard to get exclusive leads. Sites can't guarantee that consumers haven't registered at other websites, so even when you do get a lead, it might be a prospective client who has already been contacted by someone else.

PAY-PER-CLICK ADS

You can also generate leads to your website by purchasing pay-per-click (PPC) ads. If you're not paying someone else to manage your ad presence, you can pay for PPC. Google and Facebook are the two most popular sites for this type of marketing.

Typical cost per click for popular real estate terms in our market averages about $1 a click. I do not recommend spending money on general, conventional real estate keywords unless you know you'll be able to capture them as leads A typical out of the box PPC Website with IDX should be able to capture 10-20% of visitors to website as leads. The cost ranges around $12-15 per lead + monthly cost of the system itself and any ad management fees. There are certainly economies of scale as you increase your ad budget, which is why so many teams thrive on PPC leads.

The more specific the ad is—that is, the search terms whose results you purchase the space to be included with—the more effective your ad will be. For example, instead of buying an ad for "Homes for sale in Maple Grove," bid on "4 bedroom Homes for sale in Maple Grove." Specificity like this will result in less competition for this search, and thus a lower cost-per-click.

Also, the consumer searching that specific phrase has likely already narrowed down their criteria and is a more serious buyer.

A more calculated method for utilizing pay-per-click ads is to purchase long-tail keywords, and then direct the consumer to a landing page related to that topic. For instance, if someone is looking for a particular school, send them to a page about that school. Currently, in our market, there is not yet an effective way to search the MLS for topics like a school, or a specific lake or park a client may want to be near. To the extent that we can capture this type of search through keywords, we can offer more customized information for the buyer, and designate ourselves as specialists in the area where they are looking.

The most common pay-per-click (PPC) type of advertising is Google AdWords. It is straightforward to set up, and the good folks over at Google will help you for free anytime. If you're working with one of the major website providers, they most likely offer ad management included as a part of their package or may charge 10% management fee. Don't fall for companies that claim to be "Google's number one partner," or promise you a certain amount of traffic or placement. Google AdWords will help you identify potential search keywords and give you an idea of average cost per click and potential traffic.

Facebook ads are becoming much more popular for lead generation, this topic is ever changing and could fill up an entire book. If you're interested, I recommend reading the Conversion Code by Chris Smith. Otherwise, vendors such as Cuyrator, Chime, Homesnap, and BackAtYouMedia offer turnkey solutions for generating leads on Facebook.

RESOURCES

Firepoint.net

Boomtownroi.com

Commissionsinc.com

Cuyrator.com

Chime.com

Homesnap.com

BackatYouMedia.com

ORGANIC WEBSITE TRAFFIC

When it comes to generating traffic, there are two philosophies. As we discussed in the previous section, you can buy pay-per-click ads that will send people to your landing page. The second option involves attracting customers organically, by having content that comes up when people search online. This option is called search engine optimization, or SEO.

If you're serious about generating leads, in the long run, you'll need to focus on organic traffic. However, some people don't have the time or know-how to create original content and would prefer to just pay for the web traffic. While there's nothing wrong with this, you should ensure that you're getting the best bang for your buck.

You can invest millions in SEO. In reality, getting a top spot on Google is way too competitive for an individual agent. Long-tail keywords about things that are local, as we talked about in the previous section on pay-per-click, can be more likely to show up in a search engine results. Create content on your website tailored to what your audience is looking for so that when they search, your site comes up.

You can pay people to create this type of content, which may include blog posts or webpage copy. However, paying for content can backfire if the person you hire isn't knowledgeable about your region. Additionally, most services that sell content are selling you language that isn't unique to you. And consumers don't care about the generalized information delivered by this type of mass content creation. What they want to know is local information, and how it affects them. When you write and post original content, you are in control and can incorporate the details you want clients to see.

Also, when you invest in your personalized content, you will have it for years to come; it will always be working for you even after you've finished paying for it. With pay-per-click, you are spending money at a regular clip. Once your ad budget is used up, that's all you get. Ultimately, the best approach is a hybrid of the two, to drive traffic and convert leads at a successful rate.

CONTENT MARKETING

Effective content marketing is all about creating original, valuable content. A lot of people go wrong by copying and pasting others' work, or by essentially regurgitating what another expert has previously said. Also critical is to ensure that your content is relevant to your reader, and to your overall goal of selling real estate. You could write all day about your favorite movies, recipes, etc., but that will not help you sell homes.

Buyers want to read about different neighborhoods, and what amenities areas have to offer. Schools districts are of particular interest to buyers with young families, so providing buyers with quick links to boundary maps and information about the different schools in the area is very helpful. You can pair this with a jump search you've created through your broker or IDX provider. This way, when buyers are interested in a particular elementary school, they will be able to find homes in that area.

Sellers want to know what techniques you can offer to help sell their home. If homes in a particular area are selling quickly and for more money, those homeowners would be interested to read about it. Are you doing something different than your competitors to market properties? Write about it!

Consumers are out there surfing the web right now, and if you have original content to offer, they will want to read it. Content marketing for real estate is a great way to capture buyers' and sellers' attention before they enter the marketplace.

IDX

The internet database exchange, or IDX, allows you to display listings on your website. It also gives you the capability to create content, like specific pages focusing on a particular school or neighborhood, with included listings matching that topic. Most buyers use the internet to search for homes, not for agents. Offering an easy way for them to find properties will result in leads, either through a squeeze page (a page that pops up and blocks you from going further until you put in information) or from inquiries on individual listings.

There are a limited number of vendors who sell the ability to integrate data. Individual web developers can set up your website with this feature. It's best to work with a developer who is familiar with building real estate websites to ensure proper functionality. Spending more on your site pays off, both concerning the leads you're able to generate, as well as the control you have over the information you share.

Pages with embedded saved searches capture visitors' preferred search factors, which will tell you what's important to buyers. Examples include searches for information on schools, neighborhoods, new construction developments, specific condo buildings or lake homes. Having saved searches that complement your niche will promote you as an expert.

Saved jump searches combined with original content are a great way to provide value to viewers. Once the pages have been created, they will automatically update as new listings come on the market. If you aren't sure how to set this up, you can hire someone to do it for you and to train you how to make the best use of it. Services like this, while useful, can be costly, so make sure this strategy makes sense for your business before taking this leap.

RESOURCES

Real Estate Webmasters
Cuyrator

RETARGETING ADS

In this day and age, online marketing is more important than ever for real estate professionals to stand apart from the pack. Even when the market is thriving, how do you claim your share of the action? It's easy to become overwhelmed by the countless and sophisticated digital marketing tools out there, but this chapter is an excellent primer on the options available to you as a real estate professional.

THE BASICS OF RETARGETING FOR REAL ESTATE MARKETING

Let's start simple: what is retargeting? Retargeting is about meaningful reconnection with a potential client who once visited your site, but kept surfing around without committing or sharing their contact info.

Consider this: it's not uncommon to deliberate on a purchase, and ultimately walk away and decide to think about it a little longer. Retargeting finds that potential customer and puts your message in front of them again, inching them closer to closing the gap and choosing you as their real estate representation.

When it comes to potential home buyers or sellers, studies indicate that their window of web exploration usually lies between two weeks to four months. In that time, it's highly likely that a lead has explored your site but chose not to connect with you. Retargeting that lead through subtly placed ads can retrigger their interest and complete the sales funnel. When that web visitor goes browsing around the web, your retargeting efforts will stay close at hand, acting as a constant yet unobtrusive reminder of your services standing at the ready.

HOW DOES RETARGETING WORK?

Retargeting campaigns use a small piece of code called a *pixel*. Each time a visitor peruses your site, this pixel creates and inserts an anonymous "cookie"—or a bit of stored data—that stays with that visitor as they continue their web browsing. Pixels are invisible, don't affect your site's functionality, or interrupt a visitor's experience.

When a potential client visits a site where ads are present, your retargeted advertising kicks into gear and displays your ad, *keeping* you and your services at the top of his or her mind. It's important to note that pixels don't traffic in confidential user data, so there's no need to fear that you're invading your website visitors' privacy. Retargeting efforts are anonymous, and only blindly keep tabs on visitors to your site.

IS RETARGETING EFFECTIVE?

The beauty of retargeting is that ethically reinforces the fact that a potential client was in need of services that you happen to provide and visited your site to learn more. Retargeting through sites such as Facebook & AdRoll is merely a way of continuing the conversation.

You can also quickly create a custom audience on Facebook by uploading a CSV file with all of your friends, family, past clients, and leads, which will allow you to boost posts and target ads specifically to people with whom you've already been in contact and are more likely to engage with you.

House hunters and potential home sellers today almost always begin their research process online. By incorporating retargeting marketing efforts, you stay front and center where you know a need exists. Real estate agents, brokers, and business owners can't be everywhere at once, and you can't follow up on a website without contact information.

Retargeting ads make up for these shortcomings and creates new opportunities for business without eating up your time or badgering potential clients with cold-calls, spam e-mails, and the like. Retargeting is a simple, and easy way to make yourself available to clients already in search of help.

RESOURCES

AdRoll.com

Business.facebook.com

Real Estate Webmasters

Cuyrator

SIGN CALLS/LISTING INQUIRES

Every sign call is the opportunity for a new appointment. When you take on a new listing, do you ever have a wonderful feeling of excitement, waiting for that first interested call to come in? Though sign calls present an opportunity, they also offer one of the most challenging forms of leads in the real estate industry.

To convert sign calls, consider the following key moves:

QUICKLY TAKE CONTROL OF THE CONVERSATION

Within the first few seconds of the call, it's essential to put yourself in control. Sign callers generally ask about price. But, if you answer their first question immediately, it's likely that they will just hang up.

With that in mind, I invite you to consider using a stop statement, which will change the tone of the call. A stop statement affords you the opportunity to direct the conversation where you want it to go—ideally, to an appointment at your office.

When someone inquires about the property, whether about price or the number of bedrooms and bathrooms, consider incorporating the following statement: *"Thanks for your call. Allow me to look up that information that you asked for."* Using this statement puts *you* in control, giving you the opportunity to ask questions.

After using your stop statement, proceed immediately to your questions. Asking questions helps your vet the caller to determine if he or she will qualify for your services. It's important to ask questions that will lead the buyer toward your goal: bringing them to your office to meet with you, which is the best use of your time.

To convert the sign call into an appointment, concentrate on the following:

- Ask interest-piquing questions
- Avoid questions regarding bedrooms or bathrooms
- Ask questions where you will be able to anticipate their answer
- Limit your conversation to less than three minutes

Asking simple questions in a brief conversation will make it more palatable for the caller to agree to meet because you've proven that you can get to the point and are respectful of their time.

The chances of making contact with a new lead are excellent if you call no more than five minutes after submission while waiting more than thirty minutes is about 100 times less likely to end in contact.

Using a specialized number on your signs or riders, such as one from CallAction allows you to capture more information, and blast the call out to multiple team members to increase chances of making a live connection. If no one is available to answer, the system will automatically send out a text to the caller asking them when a good time to connect would be. Then you can follow-up promptly, this way you're not missing out on opportunities that don't leave a voicemail and wouldn't have likely picked up had you called back at a later time.

1. **Be sure to return all calls within 60 seconds or less.** People will remark how impressed they are that you contacted them so quickly. If the caller is a potential seller, your fast response confirms that you're a proactive, aggressive agent— precisely the kind of representative sellers need in today's market.

2. **Give callers the option of having the information about the house texted to them.** Be ready with a template that includes photos, virtual tours, videos and any supplements for the property. You can even use a text number for lead capture on your sign rider. For example

"Text '3D' to (612) 324-0516 to view photos and virtual tour" Go ahead and try it out.

3. **Be available for lead calls daily between 8 a.m. and 9 p.m.** Keep in mind that some of the best leads come in after 5 p.m.; as people are driving home from work, they'll see the new listings and call. Also, take note of when a neighbor calls in for a price-they are likely curious because they intend to list their home soon. Also, expect an increase in calls from Thursday through Sunday.

4. **Make sure everyone on the team has up to date information your listings.** Buyers expect answers, and if you have to call back to give it to them, then you may have already lost them. It's your job to know the property details and the local market.

5. **When speaking with leads, repeat and affirm everything they say**; it might feel odd at first, but it's key to building trust and getting clients to realize that you are listening and that you care. Also, use the potential client's name when speaking with them. Combine these tactics with thoughtful questions and attentive listening, and you'll earn superb results.

RESOURCES

Callaction.co

Lowen Signs

Build A Sign

HOME VALUATION LEADS

Some real estate websites allow agents to sponsor a particular Pay-Per-Click *"What is my home worth?"* ad, which leads people to a website that captures their information and gives them a sense of the value of their home. You then have their contact information and can follow up with them. They may or may not be interested in selling (or buying), but you are still meeting someone you haven't met before, and that opens doors. The goal is merely to find out what they want, and if you can provide it.

Lots of vendors offer landing pages for home valuations that are branded with your information, with a domain name that you choose. Other companies that can send out postcards and run Facebook ads include Smart Zip, GeographicFarm.com, Core Fact, and HomeValues.com.

All of these sites offer essentially the same service: driving people to landing pages, where potential leads provide information with which you may contact them.

This service usually costs around $70 per month. For a Facebook or Google PPC strategy to be successful, you'll need to invest between $500 and $2,000 per month.

CRAFTING A SUCCESSFUL LANDING PAGE TO BOOST YOUR BUSINESS

Overstating the importance of a well-cultivated online presence is difficult. When done correctly, your website should be a beacon that lures potential clients and showcases your identity and value as a business. But what about the power of landing pages? The sole purpose of these pages it to harvest contact information so that you can convert your new lead into a sale. Think of landing pages as the latest generation of directing marketing; these dedicated pages are specific calls to action. When executed with precision, landing pages often boast a high conversion rate and can boost traffic to your brand. As you craft or fine-tune landing pages for your website, keep a few of the following ideas in mind to make them as effective as possible.

KEEP IT CLEAN.

The point of a landing page is to convert targeted interest into a lead. To do this, the design and content of your landing page should be clear, organized, and cleanly designed. Avoid clutter or unnecessary copy that obscures your conversion funnel.

Make content engaging.

Sleek design creates an inviting framework, but your content should do the heavy lifting on your landing page. Pump up the keywords that drew visitors to your landing page. Organize your information with specific and engaging sub-headlines. Bulleted information that draws upon stats, testimonials, and other specifics, also makes content more readable.

Curate your Call to Action.

Since the goal of a landing page is to gather contact information as a lead, try adding an easily spotted and straightforward contact form. Also, be sure to tailor the flow of your content with conversion in mind. For instance, the theme of your landing page should be clear from the beginning and narrow in gradually on a conclusive Call to Action.

Create an incentive.

To mobilize your would-be customer, you might consider pairing your Call to Action with a promotion or incentive to submit contact information. A promo code, discount, or some bonus for signing up for your newsletter or sharing contact information can go a long way to cement the effectiveness of your Call to Action.

Incorporate visuals.

In this day and age, it doesn't hurt to supplement written content with a few visual elements. Again, it's important to keep things streamlined and clutter-free, but a well-placed infographic or image related to your product/service can break up content in an intriguing way. You can further capitalize on visuals by making them clickable, sending visitors to a more individually relevant landing page, a contact form, or a Call to Action.

As a direct marketing tool, landing pages pack a lot of power. But like any tool, they are only useful if used intelligently. If you want to make the most of your digital presence, adding well-crafted landing pages to the mix can grow your imprint and convert online interest into real-world sales. Keep these tips in mind as you curate your landing pages and bolster your business in the process.

RESOURCES

Prime Seller Leads

Geographicfarm.com

Curaytor

Lead Pages

Bold Leads

Listing2Leads

Home Value Leads

DIRECT MAIL

D irect mail is a fundamental part of your real estate marketing playbook. It is a versatile and personal method of getting the word out about your services, and why you are the best and most obvious choice. However, because direct mail is such a vital tool, it's easy to get overwhelmed when figuring out how to get started, and how to use it to get you the results you want.

FIRST THING'S FIRST: FIGURE OUT YOUR GEO-FARM

A geo-farm is a defined geographic area of households to which you send regular mailings over the course of a year, with the specific goal of increasing your number of listings. You will need to determine an area that has a high likelihood of homeownership turnover, and then create awareness and familiarity among members of that community. Through that effort, you should become a real estate agent of choice within that area.

While this is a method that takes time and commitment, it can be advantageous and have long-lasting results.

IDENTIFYING THE FARM

The first thing you'll need to do is determine your area to farm; ideally, it is close enough to your home or office that you're able to monitor the goings on there and respond quickly to provide optimal service. Many agents will farm the neighborhood they live in; however, it's worth bearing in mind that some sellers will not want a neighbor knowing their personal information.

Avoid the temptation to select an area based solely on a high price point, or because you've lived in that neighborhood and have some history there. Choosing a location for reasons like these are driven either by the misconception that more money per transaction should be your primary goal or by an emotionally-based attachment to an area. Neither motivation necessarily translates into a good foundation for your geo-farm area. You'll want to make a more thorough assessment of some critical factors to determine if a given area will likely net you a good return on your investment of time and money.

TURNOVER RATES

It's much more useful to look at the turnover rate of an area rather than home values and to assess the number of transactions you're likely to gain as a function of that rate. The turnover rate can be calculated as the number of homes sold in a neighborhood over one year, divided by the total number of homes in that neighborhood.

(Turnover rate = # of homes sold / total # of homes)

You can find this information by looking it up in the MLS, or in tax records.

Alternately, a software program called Realist allows you to search tax records for this information easily.

When you're looking at the number of homes sold in your potential farm, it's essential to use a polygon search (where you draw your own shape onto a map in the MLS system) instead of a wild card or neighborhood field – this will get more accurate results.

Because "neighborhood" is not a drop-down menu category in all MLS systems, it's not always uniformly documented. Some people will spell the neighborhood name wrong, or abbreviate, or not include it at all. When you search by polygon, the search covers everything within the boundaries of your shape, regardless of how it's categorized in the system.

Choosing where to farm based on turnover rate will give you better results. Where homes sell more often, you have a higher likelihood of getting a listing. Even though an area has high prices, if there is little turnover, you'll end up with fewer sales.

When choosing an area, ideally, you'll want to see a 6 percent turnover rate or higher. Looking at the previous year's data will be a good indicator of how many homes are likely to turn over in an area for the coming year. Sales trends can be monitored on a line graph, so as you start to see the turnover trend slowing, you might want to try farming a new area.

AVERAGE SALE PRICE

All of the above is not to say that home prices are irrelevant. You need to know the median sale price for homes in an area to assess your projected ROI. Search the MLS for areas where the average sale price is a sufficient amount to match your goal, *and* there is a decent rate of turnover.

AVERAGE DAYS ON MARKET

Another consideration that needs to go into your assessment of a potential farm area is the average number of days homes stayed on the market. A neighborhood where homes sit on the market for a long time might not be a good target as an area where homes move quickly.

Often the best areas for geo-farming are those where home styles are more homogenous because they tend to sell more quickly. In older neighborhoods where every home has unique attributes, it can take longer to find a matching buyer for your listing. Conversely, people looking in an area with mostly similar homes usually know the criteria they want and don't require one specific house because many homes in the area meet their needs.

Also, newer neighborhoods turn over faster, because initially, everyone is on the same buying cycle. Consider that people statistically move every seven to ten years. In new communities where everyone bought around the same time when the development was brand new, they will likewise be hitting the seven-year mark at about the same time. As neighborhoods get older, subsequent sales become more staggered, and turnover rates decrease because homeowners are no longer on similar buying cycles.

Another demonstrated trend is that townhouses tend to have higher turnover rates, as they typically attract more significant numbers of move-up buyers. People may have a shorter living cycle in a townhome before re-entering the market, and therefore a larger volume of sales occur in areas with concentrations of these types of homes.

SIZE OF AREA

How big should your farmed area be? You don't want to take on too big an area since it costs time and money to market to your farm regularly. But, you also don't want to select an area that is too small to give you sufficient listings to make it worth your while. A rule of thumb is to target at least 500 homes. Your farm could even be a single building containing a large number of condominium units. There is no cap on how big your farm can grow, as long as your budget and time allow you to service the area with sufficient frequency and attention.

The frequency of contact is more important than the size of your target area. Asking ten people for their business ten times yields better results than asking 100 people just once each. If a homeowner isn't thinking of selling right now, they may just toss your marketing away, and that would be a waste of your effort.

However, if you're mailing to them multiple times, two things happen. First, the consumer will begin recognizing your name, and you'll organically develop a brand as an agent who knows that neighborhood. Second, your chances of success increase proportionately to the number of times you send out marketing. The homeowner may not be selling today, but they might be three months from now.

COMPETITION

It's also worthwhile to see who else is already mailing in the area you are considering. If there is someone already dominating that market, it might not be the right place for you to focus.

For example, of the neighborhoods I researched, I determined that I could receive a 26 percent ROI in the Bonaire neighborhood. That would be great, except that I happened to know that someone from my same company was already mailing to this area. I decided that in this case, particularly in light of the small number of homes in the area and low turnover rate, the competition was just too high and not a good investment of my time and money.

FREQUENCY VS. REACH

It's important to be in touch with targets in your geo-farm on a monthly basis to become a natural resource to them. The rate at which you broadcast your message is more important than the number of people who receive it each time. Some agents will contact their targets up to 24 times per year, or every two weeks. However, we believe this level of frequency is risky: not only are you doubling your mailing budget, but you may be in danger of alienating your target audience by annoying them. We recommend twelve mailings per year, one every month.

After twelve months (and twelve mailings), I look back to see if my targeting was successful or not. I look at turnover rates, at whether sellers that did list their homes called me, what percentage of area listings I got and which homes sold. I diligently gather as much information as possible to assess how I did, giving me insights from which to make business decisions for the upcoming year. Overall, mailing areas and mailing lists will remain mostly unchanged from one year to the next, aside from dropping people who are no longer in the neighborhood. As with other strategies we talk about in this book, it's crucial that you commit to the area you've chosen to farm and not make any drastic changes for at least one year.

WHAT TO SEND

Now that you've established a geo-farm to which you'll mail at least once a month, you need to decide what to post. There are all sorts of companies out there trying to sell you marketing materials, including things like recipes, sports schedules, and seasonal/holiday items.

Don't assume that recipients will hold on to your marketing, especially your first mailing. It may fail to get someone's attention, particularly when they're not planning a move anytime soon. People are busy, and they don't look at what they consider junk mail.

Give the consumer something of value, such as market statistics for the area, or recently sold comparisons. The most useful information you can provide to home-owners is real estate-related, generally in one of three categories:

Evidence of success—e.g., a "just sold" card, noting percent of the listing price received, and days on the market;

A call to action –e.g., an announcement of buyers looking for homes, with specifics, mailed only to potential sellers meeting the sought criteria;

An invitation to your landing page—e.g., a postcard that offers to help figure out the value of their home.

You might also send other things as a gentle reminder that you are available, with a piece of advice related to homeownership, or information on a market trend.

Remember that most people are very visual, so keep your marketing consistent to strengthen your brand. Avoid sending something with little to no value, such as a card with your branding but no content.

It's best to alternate your messages each month, rotating consistently through each of the above categories. Vendors can help you coordinate your messaging. The additional cost of using a vendor is offset by the decreased cost per unit based on the volume of postcards being mailed.

Just Listed & Just Sold postcards are potent marketing tools. Real estate often has a popcorn effect, in which multiple homes in one neighborhood go on the market at the same time soon after one home is listed.

A rush of new listings such as this is a great time to demonstrate your expertise in the area and gives the neighbors a taste of your professional marketing. Once the home sells, let the neighbors know with a Just Sold card, and be sure to ask for their business.

All of your marketing should suggest that you're an expert in the area and at that particular price point. It should provide examples of instances where you successfully marketed a home and attracted qualified buyers.

Did you overcome any challenges during the transaction? Were there multiple offers? Did you receive an offer close to or above the original list price? Were you able to sell it in fewer days than the average for your market? Did you do something unique to market the property? These are all things that make great attention getters for your Just Sold cards.

There should also be a clear call to action, along with your contact information. You'd be surprised by how many agents overlook that detail.

At the end of the year, I sort our sales by style, location, and price point to create postcards that feature anywhere from six to eight similar properties. Each card has a photo, a caption describing the property, the percent list-to-sale price, and its days on the market. We do not use actual listing or sales price because it is irrelevant. The consumer may have a preconceived idea of the value of their home. What is essential is to illustrate how close we were to the actual sales price and how quickly the seller was able to move on.

You should also be sending these same messages out via your website and social media. Photos, stories, and testimonials from clients are very effective ways to advertise.

BEST PRACTICES FOR CALLS TO ACTION

When designing the content of your mailing, one crucial component is to include a compelling ***call to action (CTA)***—how you're asking your audience to engage, in a manner that invites them to receive value from you and deepens their association with you and your service.

One of the best ways to frame your CTA is to make it specific. Rather than sending a card saying generally, "Homes Sold Recently in Your Neighborhood," give details indicating your success with aspects consumers care about, such as what percent of the list price you got, and how many days the home was on the market. Showcase your prior successes in that neighborhood, and you position yourself to be the agent of choice in the future.

All your marketing pieces need to have consistent branding and represent the level of professionalism you provide. Use professional photography and maintain some common visual elements across all of your mailings to build familiarity; this will encourage people to trust your expertise and to take action when they are ready.

One good strategy is to invite people to find out information about the price of their home by giving them a website through which to input their data. Asking them to go online and check it out for themselves is a strong call to action, and a more effective prompt than merely telling them their home's value in a mailer.

Another conventional approach is to send a mailer stating, "Thinking of selling?" or, "We have buyers looking for homes in your neighborhood." A much better CTA for this type of message would be to provide additional details and specificity that connects the audience with your request: "I have a homebuyer, Frank, looking for a home with three to four bedrooms and two stories, in the Southview school district." Then, only send this mailer to homes matching those criteria. People are much more likely to follow up on that kind of solicitation. Evoking your reader's emotion gets a higher response rate.

I also like to send personal invites to my open houses within my geo-farm. If there's another agent in your office with a listing in your geo-farm, ask them if it would be okay to hold an open house there on their behalf.

CHECKLIST FOR A SUCCESSFUL MAILING:

- ☐ Did you provide something of value (market statistics, recently sold comparisons, etc.)?
- ☐ Did you include a call to action with your contact information?
- ☐ Does your mailing piece reflect your brand?
- ☐ Is it visually appealing?
- ☐ Does your piece position you as an expert in the area and price point you're targeting?
- ☐ Did you alternate your messaging each month?

WORKING WITH A VENDOR

As we've noted, homeowners will statistically move an average of every seven years, which is very easy to track using public tax records. We can also use public records to look up how much they paid and use automated value systems to have an idea of what their home might be worth now.

You want to focus your marketing efforts on those who may be ready, willing, and able to sell. It doesn't make a lot of sense to market to someone who just bought their house, or who is upside down on their mortgage.

Consider the reasons people decide to sell: it might be a promotion, marriage, a new addition to the family, job relocation, graduation, divorce, or death. Most real estate sales occur because of a significant life change. The more tuned in you are to your geo farm, the quicker you can anticipate these changes, and prepare yourself to get in front of the sellers at the right time.

Companies such as Corefact.com and GeographicFarm.com can help you set up your farm and have automated mailing programs designed for real estate. These vendors include a Seller Landing Page to collect interested homeowners' information and provide them with an estimated value. You could also create your postcards and drive traffic to a landing page from a company like Prime Seller Leads, or HomeValues.com

With a geo-farm, your average success rate should be about one in 2,000 contacts, meaning that for every 2,000 physical pieces of mail, you will likely see one closed transaction. Vendors will try to sell you on a promised "response rate," but there can be some confusion between annual response rates and per-mailer response rates. To assess how you're doing, look at your *success rate* on a yearly basis relative to how many pieces of mail you sent.

METHODS OF MAILING

Not all mailing methods are created equal. In fact, there is some truth to the adage "you get what you pay for." It's a good idea to consider *how* you mail when you send out your geo-farm mailings.

First Class	Business Class	Bulk Mail
- More expensive - You stamp and address - Will receive the bounce-backs	- Less costly - Large delivery time window - More danger of being lost in junk mail	- Cheapest - Goes to everyone on the carrier's route

For your first mailing to an area, you should spend the extra money to put stamps on the envelopes, and either hand-address or print a label, so that your mail will go *first class*. This way, you'll get the bounce-back—all the items with undeliverable addresses. Many agents don't realize that you won't get your returned mail with bulk mailing. Getting this returned mail is essential because you can use it to refine your list, fix errors, and scrub the wrong addresses. If you don't do this, you could spend the next year paying for mail to go repeatedly right into the dead letter garbage.

After you've scrubbed your list, use the business class rate to send your mailings. You won't get the bounce

-back, and there is a pretty broad delivery time window with this type of mail. Often, carriers will deliver all business mail on the same day of the week, so people receive a lot of junk mail all at once, meaning that your fabulous postcard is less likely to get noticed and more likely to get tossed in the trash. But the price differential is pretty significant between first and business classes. It doesn't pay to use first class unless it's your first mailing to the area, or you're sending something that is time sensitive.

The third class of mail is called "Every Door Direct Mail" (EDDM), and this is what we refer to as bulk mail. EDDM, as its name suggests, goes to everyone on a given carrier's route. Each piece in a mass mailing will be considerably cheaper, but you'll need to weigh the cost savings against the lack of specificity to your selected audience.

Often, by making a targeted list, you can cut the number of people in an EDDM area in half. On the other hand, if you can pinpoint a delivery route that entirely or mostly overlaps with your targeted area, it might make sense to save money this way.

Although we've touched on a lot of different methods of direct mail and its best practices, we've only exposed the tip of the iceberg. The most important takeaways here are that your geo-farm is the foundation of your direct mail campaign, and that to get the most ROI of your direct mail, give it a least a year before making any drastic changes.

Resources

GeographicFarm.com

CoreFact.com

Remine.com

Eddm.usps.com

DOOR KNOCKING

Does door-knocking really work? If you do a Google search of "door-knocking for real estate agents," you'll find countless success stories. Stories like Tom Mitchell with Keller Williams, who in 2013 closed $38.8 million in home sales, all from door-knocking and Shannon Brooks with Engel & Volker's, who closed 26 transactions her first year in business, eight of which she attributes to door-knocking.

Plain and simple: *yes,* door-knocking does work. Then why don't more agents utilize this strategy?

We will come up with every excuse under the sun not to door knock, we say we don't have time yet we'll spend hours on Facebook, Instagram or Pinterest. I've heard agents say no one will be home, or I don't want to interrupt their dinner. Heaven forbid some actually answer the door, and you have to talk to them. I get it, door knocking isn't for everyone and if you fall into that category of people, by all means, feel free to move onto the next chapter.

TIPS FOR PRODUCTIVE DOOR-KNOCKING

Agents who find successes with door-knocking follow a few essential rules:

- Dress appropriately for your market. If you sell real estate in casual Huntington Beach, California, for example, you don't want to wear a shirt and tie. But in New York City, you'd be wise to consider it.

- Smile. This should go without saying, but you might be surprised at how difficult it can be when you're nervously approaching your first few doors.

- Stay back from the door three feet or so.

- Bring something to leave with the homeowner—make sure the material is branded with your information. RPR (REALTOR® Property Resource, provided by NAR) has some incredibly consumer-friendly home and community reports you can leave with the homeowner.

- Be target-specific. Area, style, price range, and audience are important when choosing where you want to door-knock. In some markets, agents have access to data that can be helpful.

For instance, Realist* allows you to identify an area using a map search, which enables you to set specific criteria to find homes where the owner has lived in the house for a certain amount of time. It also gives you the original sale price, which you can use to determine the homeowner's amount of equity.

— Be consistent. There's a chance that on your first time out, or your tenth or your hundredth, you will end up empty-handed. *Keep going!*

SCRIPTS: CONSISTENCY COUNTS

Get familiar enough with your script that you don't sound canned, but conversational and organic so you can concentrate on listening to your potential client, and not on when it's your turn to speak. Like all lead generation techniques, the results from knocking on doors takes time to illustrate what kind of return on investment you are getting. Remember, this is a marathon, not a sprint! It can take from three to six months to see results, so use a schedule to keep yourself on task. It is crucial that you commit time and consistency if you hope to reap lucrative rewards.

Then, as with all lead generation methods, the fortune is in the follow-up. Send a thank-you note about a week after a conversation with a homeowner. Add the names and notes to your CRM system and choose your action plan. Typical follow-up plans include newsletters, market update emails, additional personal touches, calls and direct mail.

Keep in mind that you are always knocking on some kind physical or mental door, and your level of success and happiness depends on how good you are at getting through those doors, and how consistent you are at overcoming your doubts and anxieties.

Last tip: Set a goal to knock on a specific number of doors per week as part of your larger marketing plan. Track your success and failures, so you know what's working, and where you need to tweak your efforts.

RESOURCES

Realtor Property Resource
Infosparks
MLS Market Data
Just List, Just Sold, Open House information

EXPIRED LISTINGS

Expired listings are a great option because those sellers have already raised their hands and announced to the world that they want to sell. For most of these homeowners, the need to sell is still urgent, and many are wary of going through the process again of finding another agent to represent them. Most do not know why their home did not sell, but they are frustrated with their previous agent and, sometimes, with all agents. They will rarely return to the agent that failed to sell their home.

Your job is to figure out how to get in front of them and secure a listing appointment. Whether that is by knocking on a homeowner's door, dropping off valuable information, writing a compelling letter, or calling the seller relentlessly. Before you get too excited, be sure to check if the sellers have already relisted as occasionally agents will do a cancel relist as a marketing strategy. Nothing will make you look more foolish (and unethical) then marketing to a property that has already been relisted. During a seller's market when inventory is in short supply expect a lot of agents to be pursuing these sellers using various tactics, some may claim to have a buyer for the home, others are quick to discount their commission. Be sure to understand your value proposition as an agent and position yourself as the expert whom has what it takes to get their property sold.

Years ago we would mail out a three-part letter to listings in the area that had expired and would consistently get about 1 in 50 or so to call and schedule an appointment with us. Now that the market has changed there are a lot more aggressive agents pursuing these opportunities, we still do get appointments but not nearly at the rate we use to. I've had sellers tell me they've received upwards of 50 pieces of mail and a handful of phone calls when their property went off the market despite being on the do not call list. They've expressed feelings of being overwhelmed and put off by some of the agent's efforts. If you're coming from a place of service, and are comfortable with your follow up methods expired listings can still be a great source of business.

Until the property is relisted, it is a potential listing lead that should be nurtured just like any other lead. Our first letter introduces our team and details of how we conduct business. Subsequently, we follow up and offer tips and suggestions that have helped other sellers in the past sell their homes quickly. Many agents stop after the first mailer or unanswered phone call, you'll want to continue to follow up. Some of the best opportunities may be homes that expired 2-3 years ago, check your MLS and see if you can find ones that haven't relisted.

If you decide you're going to call be sure to be consistent, block out time each day for your calls, and make several attempts to contact the seller before giving up. Don't assume they will remember that you called because they won't, they may even confuse you with one of the other agents they've spoken to. It is absolutely crucial that you secure a meeting in person.

Ask the seller what the other agent did to market their property. Gain an understanding of the owner's expectations regarding the time frame, listing price, sales price, and access for showings, as well as their interest in the evaluation of the competition they face in the current marketplace.

Use your track record to gain credibility with the owners. Supply references of satisfied clients, especially those clients whose listings were also expired before you began working with them.

When we found our letters were not working as well as they were previously we tried adding phone calls. At first, a member of our team said they'd take responsibility and would call expired listings every day, so I sought out to find the best data source and dialer. We tried Arch Agent, Landvoice, Mojo Dialer and RedX, each had its own little quirks. We noticed that homes that were moved to contingent status or temporarily not available for showing would come up on the list as expired, there were issues with data feeds, and invalid numbers which were certainly frustrating. Weeks after we got all of the kinks worked out that team member was discouraged with the lack of results, so they gave up on calling completely. This left me with a system, but no time of my own to call on them, so we decided to outsource to a call center. That too came with its share of challenges which we had to overcome, we did end up getting additional listing appointments and won business that we would not have gotten without the calls. However at the end of the day, we didn't feel that it fit in well with our business model, so we discontinued the service of those products and stopped using the virtual assistant. This isn't to say that the process doesn't work, there are lots of agents out there that have mastered this lead generation technique.

Our team's experience with expired listings illustrates the ongoing challenges of building an economy-proof real estate business, as well as the need for diversification of your approach. If my team had been in a position where we relied too heavily on our expired listing success, this recent change in the market would have hit us hard. Instead, we have turned our focus to other strategies which continue to yield good results.

Diversifying our strategies this way underscores the importance of continually tweaking your practices. All strategies need regular review—don't assume that because one approach was very successful in the past that it will always be successful.

RESOURCES

Arch Agent
Landvoice
Mojo Dialer
RedX

FSBO

For Sale By Owner listings are similar to those that have expired. However, these sellers have decided to go it on their own, often as an attempt to save money. Some mistakenly believe that all they need to do is hastily make a sign and stick it in the front yard, and they'll get the house sold without having to deal with an agent. Others are savvy enough to have put the listing on portals such as Zillow, or may have hired a company to put the home on MLS for them but are trying to manage the transaction themselves.

You can identify opportunities in For Sale by Owner listings by searching online or driving around and looking for yard signs. Sellers who opted to list their home themselves may place ads on online marketplaces such as Craiglist, Nextdoor, and Facebook. Occasionally you'll find that they're also already listed on the MLS or that it is actually an unethical agent or vendor posing as a seller to generate leads. Zillow allows homeowners to list their home via the "Make Me Move" feature. Recent data reports that most buyers don't use this feature to find a property as they have to opt-in, and with the tons of listings already there isn't much reason to do so. Sellers using MMM often go long stretches of time without any serious interest, they may be inundated with commercial requests, or struggle with logistics of showing homes to those who inquired online. If you've ever sold anything on craigslist or Facebook Marketplace, you should know how frustrating it can be when a potential buyer simply doesn't show up.

ONCE I'VE FOUND THEM, THEN WHAT?

Do your homework and research not only the property, but the seller as well – a little googling on your lead might feel a bit like stalking, but you are merely doing your due diligence. Make sure you are dealing with someone that you'd like to help, and that you are pursuing a property that has a chance of improving your business.

Don't be easily discouraged – an FSBO lead might be quick to turn you down, but don't take it personally. They might be seeing the idea of hiring an agent as a kind of failure on their part, and thus have an extra-high wall of resistance to your services.

To earn their trust, offer some free advice, leave your card or contact info, and follow up with them like you would any other lead. The ones that come to see the sense of hiring you will find their way back to you in due time.

Once you've identified an FSBO that you can work with, it's your time to show off your skills at market analysis. Gently inform the seller that finding the right price is far more complicated than they might think, and let them know that they could actually make more money on the sale with your help.

Consider developing specific scripts for this category of follow-up that explore the seller's frame of mind. Below are some questions that you might want to ask:

1. *"If I brought you a qualified buyer, would you be willing to pay me a (% commission that you are comfortable with)?"* If the response is a firm "no," then this seller might not be ready to entertain ideas of going with an agent, and you might be better off simply stepping away, but keeping an eye on the listing to see if it continues to linger on the market. If the answer is yes, or if the seller seems to imply that they are considering the idea, continue on to the next question.

2. *"How long are you going to try to sell your home on your own before considering other options?"* Notice that you are not asking when they are going to give up and hire an agent; the seller retains the idea that they are still in control here. The response to this answer is often telling – if they say around two months, there's a fair chance that they will list in a month. If the answer is six months or less, that is an excellent opportunity to continue to the next question.

3. ***"If you don't sell your home by that time, what other options will you consider?"*** This is a great chance to find out if they have a friend or relative who is an agent that they are considering giving the listing to if their FSBO dreams don't work out. You don't want to waste time and effort pursuing leads that already have an agent in mind. If the seller responds that they are open to interviewing agents in the future, leave your contact info and fold them into your follow-up campaign.

4. The keys to success with FSBO listings are research and follow-up. A little homework and a tactful way to share the data to back up why listing with you is the way to go will help you get the listings you're after.

RESOURCES

Zillow Make Me Move

Craigslist

Nextdoor

Facebook Marketplaces

PROBATE SALES

Probate is the process by which a deceased person's assets are divided up, this often includes real estate. Often times those heirs will need to sell the property to pay off liabilities, or to split up proceeds amongst surviving relatives.

Not many agents you talk to will be pursuing probate sales as a source of business, this may be because it comes with the stigma of being considered an ambulance chaser. Most aren't even aware of where to find these opportunities much less have a strategy for pursuing them. As with any of the other strategies covered in this book, for every naysayer that discounts marketing to the family of deceased homeowners I can point out several real estate professionals who have built their career helping those families.

If you do decide to pursue probate as a marketing strategy, the first step is to identify the opportunities. Information about probate proceedings are filed at the county and include the deceased's name, last known address, the executor of the estate, and if applicable the attorney involved. You can also purchase this information from companies such as AllTheLeads.com, usprobateleads.com, or successorsdata.com Expect to pay $200-300/month per county, the benefit is that the information has been scrubbed and often appended with additional contact information.

The three top methods of prospecting probate leads, mailing directly to the home, mailing to the executor of the estate, and building relationships with attorneys who specialize in probate sales. I'm a big fan of building relationships, especially with those who have the ability to steer business your way. For more on that read the chapter dedicated to networking.

Since the probate process can be lengthy, it is likely that the home has sat vacant for some time, the family members may have already been in contact with an agent and been solicited by investors looking for a good deal. Your job is to become the specialist, an expert on the process, provide recommendations for vendors, and be an unbiased, neutral party to all heirs. Though ultimately the executor of the estate will have the final say, it is important to be respectful of each family member's opinions and projected outcome for sale of the property.

Letters mailed to the home or to the executor of the estate should introduce you as a local professional whom understands the process, and is available to provide advice as needed. I recommend sending 3 separate letters over 3 months if you're comfortable following up on the phone after each letter that will increase your success dramatically. The follow-up letters build off of the introduction and provide additional value to the recipients. Just remember it is about them not, but be sure to include some testimonials when appropriate. AllTheLeads.com offers a templated letter service that is very reasonably priced and can be completely automated. If you do automate this process be sure to cancel the 2nd and 3rd letter as you inevitably get a few that bounce back, or receive responses indicating they're not interested.

I didn't feel comfortable, nor did I have the time to make the follow-up calls, so I tried outsourcing that portion of the program to a 3rd party, as we experienced with the expired listings the results were not that great. We had more people upset that we were calling and put off by the calls then opportunities so eventually we shut it down. The letters and the calls did result in additional appointments and closed business, so the strategy certainly does work. In the end, we decided to concentrate on other aspects of our business, but I would definitely recommend giving it a shot if you're comfortable making the calls yourself.

RESOURCES

AllTheLeads.com

SuccessorsData.com

OPEN HOUSES

When it comes to pioneering a successful real estate business, you should never underestimate the power of the open house. On one front, staging an open house satisfies the seller and stirs up potential buyers.

Beyond that, an open house is also a rare marketing opportunity for you, where you and your services enjoy face-to-face time with a host of potential future clients. Holding a fruitful open house is something of an art form; below, you'll find a few critical methods to help make your next open house a memorable one.

PROMOTE CREATIVELY

To make a splash with your open house, you must drive traffic to the property. Just posting a simple sign in the front yard a few days beforehand won't drum up a significant number of visitors. Instead, focus your efforts on cross-promotion, including on online platforms, to maximize the number of visitors—and potential clients—who will be intrigued enough to visit the property.

Identify a few unique characteristics of the property, then highlight those in your promotional materials. By doing so, you attract specialized buyers more likely to take a serious interest in the property. Likewise, your efforts will make your open house stand out among the more blandly marketed set.

WORK A TIMELINE

Wise real estate agents know that the days leading up to your open house are just as important as the day of the event. Use the preceding days to knock on the doors of the homes in the neighborhood. Not only are you being courteous, but you can also spread the word regarding the open house, network within the community, encourage neighbors to invite family and friends, and potentially make a connection with a future client.

Also, use this preliminary time to scope out online listings in the area that are hosting their own open houses—posting some of your signs nearby may draw house-hunting traffic your way.

FORGE A PERSONAL CONNECTION

The day of the open house has finally arrived. How do you prepare? For starters, dressing to impress sends a message to potential buyers and future clients that you are professional and put-together.

Secondly, when engaging with visitors, try to establish a positive narrative that goes beyond the typical sales-pitch: perhaps Google has excellent restaurant recommendations for this neighborhood, or maybe you've researched the local Walk Score or school system.

Also remember to provide a means for visitors to contact you, such as an e-mail list, a sign-in sheet, or a feedback form. Finally, follow up after the fact; a thank-you note for visiting, or a friendly e-mail summarizing the property's features is an excellent way to cement a connection with a potential client.

Planning and hosting an impressive open house is no small feat. Attention to detail, preparedness, and care are all essential attributes in a successful real estate agent; these qualities are just as critical to hosting a noteworthy open house event. Use these tips to your advantage the next time you stage an open house and witness your real estate business reap the rewards.

Open Houses have long been an efficient way to assure the seller of the interest in their home, as well as to engage potential buyers. But frankly, few sales are made at an open house, and usually, the real benefit goes to the agent running it. Through thoughtful marketing and promotion, an open house is an excellent opportunity to reach an audience of 15,000 people over the three-to-four-day period before the open house.

Although virtually all real estate agents will throw or participate in many open houses in the course of their careers, most agents have not perfected the art of the open house. Putting out a few "open house" signs three minutes before the scheduled start time of the event is not going to produce the necessary results to make you successful.

If done with purpose and consistency, an open house can serve the needs of both the seller and the buyer. And perhaps most significantly, you, the agent, can register more face-to-face time engaging potential clients.

When considering an open house, make sure it is the best use of time for your business. Questions to ask yourself, or your team, include:

Is the home in my target price and area?
Does this event give me more visibility?
Is this house a good representation of my brand?
Is the house priced right?
Each of these questions will help you determine if an open house will benefit your business.

RESOURCES

Open House Pro
Realtors Property Resource®
Homesnap

HOME BUYER & SELLER
SEMINARS

In theory, buyer/seller seminars, and similar presentation-based events are a perfect way to engage people beyond your sphere. But like many of the topics we have discussed, a successful seminar is the culmination of methods and metrics.

Why Do a Seminar?

Developing new clients is not an easy task. However, by doing seminars, you have an opportunity to showcase your professionalism, market knowledge, and genuine desire to help your attendees navigate the home buying or selling process. A well-planned and executed seminar will deliver new prospects to your pipeline at a cheaper cost than many other engagement strategies.

TOPICS

What would compel *you* to attend a seminar? Chances are, it would need to be more enticing than, "Come Learn About the Buying Process," or " Thinking of Selling? Come to this Selling Seminar." Be specific and innovative when picking a topic. Some ideas include:

Neighborhood-Specific Topics: New developments, or an expansion of existing development, pique the interest of potential buyers. National builders love to showcase their products and will often agree to participate in seminars, as well as to register as attendees under the organizing agents.

Fixer-Upper Topics: Many of the homes you show to buyers are in need of repairs. Most of these fixes are easy and relatively inexpensive. However, many first-time homebuyers find these repairs daunting. Invite an inspector to explain which home repair projects are a big deal, and which aren't. Follow that up with a handyman who can give a few step-by-step instructions to fix common issues.

Home Seller Topics: Help sellers understand how to prepare their home to sell. I once did a neighborhood tour with six homeowners. At the time, none of them were committed to selling. I invited them personally, by door-knocking, asking if they were aware of what their home was worth and if they knew how their home stacked up against homes in the area. I showed them four homes within a half-mile and asked them to fill out a form on each. After, I asked each group to rate how their house compared to the homes I'd shown, using price, condition and curb appeal. This exercise resulted in a better-educated seller!

Age-Related Topics: Age is often part of the reason people decide to buy or sell. Downsizing can be rewarding, but also tricky. Helping aging homebuyers determine the benefits of selling, and assisting with a transition plan centered on their lives, is critical. Include investment advisors, estate planning attorneys, and active senior consultants to add validity to your seminar.

Yes, You CAN buy a House Topics: Geared at renters and those with past credit concerns. Explain the economics of homeownership and have a credit expert talk about overcoming credit issues such as bankruptcy or a prior foreclosure.

Relocating Buyers/Corporate Buyers And Sellers. Companies in your community are always growing and shrinking. While prospecting, call on human resource departments and ask if they will give you access to their employees. If a company is hiring, they may be willing to allow you the opportunity to provide an event helping familiarize employees with the benefits of buying. On the other hand, a company that's downsizing has employees that may need to relocate and might be willing to recommend your services.

TIMING

The date and time of your presentation are essential to consider and will determine the attendance at your seminar. Depending on your audience, time of day and time of year will draw different crowds.

First, identify your audience. Consider the time of year, such as tax time for an investor seminar, end of school year for families, or in colder or warmer climates, consider late fall for snowbirds.

Time of day depends on your audience as well. Evenings may draw 9-5 workers, while Saturdays may be more attractive to those with families, or second- and third-shift employees. A seminar geared toward aging homeowners is probably best held during the day.

LOCATION

The location or venue of your seminar has to target the audience you're trying to attract. Estimate attendance based on the topic and amount of promotion you plan to do for the event.

Plan to hold the seminar at a venue other than your office. Potential buyers and sellers are more likely to attend events held at common ground venues. They are also more likely to see the event as more valuable than just a sales pitch.

There are numerous options for venues, and many are inexpensive, or even free. Consider churches, community centers, schools or libraries. Midrange venues include restaurants, coffee shops with ample space, and hotel meeting spaces. For affluent audiences, you should consider presenting in higher-end spaces, such as yacht clubs and country clubs. For audiences with specific interests, consider places like sporting facilities, breweries, or parks.

PROMOTION

You have the topic, the speakers, the time, and the place. Now, make sure your promotion hits its mark. Many local newspapers will run stories or calendars announcing events. Contact the local press and find out how to submit information. Larger businesses may be willing to post flyers on their company bulletin boards or mention the event in their newsletter.

If you plan to pay for advertising, focus on publications and websites that are popular with people in your target audience. For instance, while targeting first-time buyers, put ads in apartment-finder publications, or send direct mail to apartment complexes. Facebook now allows agents using their promotion tool to target more specific audiences, as well as to post reminders regarding an event.

However, you promote your event, be sure to assess your investment relative to your anticipated return. Track your costs and results over time. Also, ask event attendees where they learned about your event, to help you determine what efforts are most effective.

THE EVENT ITSELF

The actual presentation is often the component that is the hardest for agents. Think about what format will be most appealing to your prospects, and who will do the best job of covering the topic in an entertaining yet informative way.

THINGS TO CONSIDER:

Will you be the expert? If so, how will you speak to the crowd: lecture-style, or with an interactive format?

Will you bring in guest speakers? (Think service providers, inspectors, credit specialists, mortgage professionals, title professionals, contractors, etc.)

Will you act as the moderator?

What audio-visual elements will you use?

Will you have handouts?

Will you offer refreshments?

Will you and your service providers field questions from the audience?

How will you allocate time?

In the end, you want your attendees to walk away with some new and useful information, and you want them to associate you with the next steps they take toward buying or selling.

Be sure to capture attendee contact information, and, as with everything in our profession, be diligent with your efforts in following up after your event. Within one day after the event, reach out to everyone who attended; request feedback on the seminar, offer to answer any additional questions they may have and explore where they are in their buying or selling process. Add these individuals into your database for continued follow-up, and circle back regularly.

RESOURCES

Eventbrite.com
Meetup.com

PRINT ADVERTISING

According to media tracking site eMarketer, magazines, newspapers, and direct mail constituted only 11% of all ad dollars spent on advertising in 2017. And it's no wonder, what with the prevalence of online ads that fit any budget and can do most of the work of finding qualified potential clients for you. However, despite the weakened reach of traditional print ads, there is still a place for them in your real estate marketing plan.

Before you jump in, here are some factors to consider.

COST OF PRODUCTION

Print and Magazine ads require the use of a graphic designer and photographer to fit the specifications on running ads. Your piece will need to be created in multiple formats depending on the platform. Photos and artwork that will appear in a full-color print format will require high definition images.

Similarly, direct mail involves an investment of time and money to create its content and develop its layout and distribution.

You may need to outsource the creation of your ad or direct mailing if you do not have the skills or the time to create material.

ADVERTORIALS

Many magazine and newspaper platforms offer an advertising vehicle known as an Advertorial. An advertorial is an article laid out to look like any other article in the magazine or newspaper except that you pay to place it there. By law, it must be labeled as an Advertorial since the FTC has strict rules regarding disclosure for paid articles.

The benefit is that it is long-form content and allows you the room to convey your message adequately. You can also include photos, charts, or other graphics. The downside is that it is labeled as an Advertorial and a reader might skip past it as they would any other ad.

CHOOSE THE RIGHT PUBLICATION.

Your first step is to study the magazines in your market and figure out which is most likely to be read by the clientele you want to reach.

Start with magazines about your region; if you live in a metroplex, the chances are good that there is a dedicated magazine about the goings on in your area.

An effective ad for your services in a locally-dedicated magazine could pique interest from people who could set up an appointment with you. Also, these magazines can be purchased by people who are preparing for a move to your area and are on the lookout for someone to help them relocate.

Another idea is to place ads in magazines about interests that your target market may participate in. For example, if your target market is the outdoors type, put an ad in a local magazine about outdoor activities that highlight your ability to find homes with lots of room for equipment.

Examine the Publication's Circulation.

Once you've determined where to run your ad, you'll want to learn everything about the magazine's reach. To do this, ask a sales rep or obtain a copy of the magazine to learn about circulation numbers, distribution areas, pricing and market image.

Regarding circulation, pay close attention to direct subscribers, because many magazines sold in markets, convenience stores and the like languish on the shelves and are never sold. Also, pay attention to the magazine's market image; while a particular magazine may have a lower circulation, if it is well-respected it may serve your needs better than a publication with more significant numbers but an overall lower image score.

Place Your Ad Strategically.

Your budget will determine where you'll place your ad. Bigger budgets will be able to claim those positions that offer the furthest reach, like near the table of contents or the page opposite a relevant article. However, sometimes you can get away with spending less by placing your ad next to a more prominent one, thereby "piggybacking" on the substantial eye traffic.

Know the Appropriate Amount of Text for Your Audience.

In theory, print ads are always short and sweet, but that rule isn't set in stone. If you know your target market well enough, you probably have a good idea of how much text it will take to get their attention.

Create Compelling Headlines.

No matter the length of the text in your ad or mailing, you must immediately grab the reader's attention. Create concise, compelling headlines that address the specific needs or desires of your target audience.

Maximize Your Budget.

Getting the best ROI for print advertising ultimately means making your budget work harder by doing extensive research. The most cost-effective ads are placed with the most information about the publication's schedule. This kind of knowledge will help you sync your ad placement to readership and business cycles. Obtaining a media kit will give you rate information as well as the magazine's reach.

TEST, MONITOR, & ADJUST.

Track the effectiveness of each ad and mailing. Do not repeat ads with low results and invest more in your higher performers. Experiment with layout and content in your mailings to learn what's working, and what isn't.

While print advertising is no longer the powerhouse it once was, it deserves consideration when building your real estate business. At the very least, experiment with it and closely track your results; the information may surprise you.

RADIO ADVERTISING

Before we jump in, I'd like to give a quite shout out to Chris Watters of Watters International Realty and author of *The Million Dollar Real Estate Team How I Went from Zero to Earning $1 Million After Expenses in Three Years,* he was kind enough to share his insights on radio advertising. If you haven't read his book yet, I highly recommend you check it out.

Once upon a time, radio was the top platform for delivering advertising messages. Radio enjoyed being in this top spot until 1941, with the debut of the first-ever televised ad. Ever since radio has struggled to claim its fair share of the advertising industry. Forecasted numbers reported by eMarketer is that radio makes up only 2% of all advertising budgets, and will continue to decrease.

For you, this has both good and bad implications when considering advertising your real estate services on the radio. First, the bad: listenership has been in steady decline over the last few decades; the average listener is approaching advanced age, and few are tuning in to replace them.

Now, however, the good: most stations, especially small regional ones, have lowered the cost of advertising in an attempt to keep advertisers and hopefully entice new ones. For this reason, radio advertising should be an option for you.

With the advent and proliferation of podcasts and other streaming services, you have many options of where to place an ad on audio or radio. There are countless opportunities to sponsor podcasts and place digital ads on the online pages that host podcasts. You can also put ads on Satellite Radio and streaming radio services.

WHERE RADIO IS STILL EFFECTIVE

Radio advertising is prime for targeting sellers agented 40-65, it has a higher proportion of that demographic that still tunes in to listen on average of 15-25 minutes per day, typically during drive-time hours for the morning and afternoon rush. Any ad you purchase should, therefore, air during those timeslots. Chris Watters cautions not to skimp out here, you need to pay for the prime time spots. He also recommends only focusing on sellers, your goal is to get them to call and say "Come list my house." The difference between success and failure for a radio advertising campaign depends entirely on preparation and planning. Radio ads are reasonably simple to create (as opposed to TV Ads), but in reality, they are marketing tools that require just as much careful analysis and planning as the most complicated campaigns.

STRATEGY & PLANNING

Strategy is the name of the game if you commit all of your funds to just one form of radio advertising you limit your chances of success. A better approach is to strategize and coordinate your radio ads with other marketing efforts, such as print ads, online marketing, and social media initiatives. You should have a consistent message across all mediums and a very strong call to action that utilizes one of your unique value propositions such as a guaranteed sale.

Radio advertising isn't for everyone, do not even consider it as a form of marketing unless you've mastered lead conversion and have 12 months of reserves in the bank. Most agents at this point will have a team, or at the very least an assistant and have consistently earned over 300k in annual GCI if you can't afford to go all in do not even dip your toe in the water.

SCRIPTING & MESSAGE

The ad must convey the "voice" of your company and services. If you have your own creative team, you may work with them, although it might be worth hiring an agency or even to work with the radio station directly to create the radio spots.

You will still need to ensure that the team you work with can stay on message for your brand. If you hire on-air talent for the ad, make sure their persona and personality are in alignment with your brand. Avoid controversial on-air personalities, and do a deep-dive into their social media habits before hiring them to convey your message to potential clients. Testimonials and endorsements on the radio go a long way, you can even get a celebrity endorsement by signing up with RATE at www.radioandtelevisionexperts.com

ANALYZE, TEST, & ADJUST

Some radio campaigns are successful right from the start. But most of the time, you will need to adjust your ads and your strategy as you go along. Make sure you have access to adequate analytical tools. Try A/B testing for a couple of ads. Vary the script and message style to see which ad garners better results. Then, apply what you've learned by investing in the more successful ads. Be sure to use a dedicated phone number such as one from CallAction so that you're able to track and respond to a high volume of incoming calls. According to Chris, once you've got everything up and running, you can expect a 6-7x ROI on a 6-month cash conversion cycle.

PAID RADIO SHOWS

Another opportunity that some radio stations have made available is the ability to build and host your radio show. These are typically 30 or 60-minute shows and usually relegated to non-peak listening hours.

These shows tend to run on weekend mornings or late nights and early mornings before 6 am.

Usual costs include paying for a producer and engineer to keep the show running smoothly. You need to pay royalties for any jingles or music played on the show, which is why most who take advantage of this option choose a talk-show format. Production costs vary, but typically start out around $3000 per episode, and go up from there.

Some stations will negotiate a package deal if you commit to multiple episodes. These shows usually run once per week. Some stations will allow you to sell advertising spots during your show where you will have to split a percentage of the monies paid. Others may not let you sell ads at all, and will instead program their regular advertising schedule, keeping all the revenue.

This more extended format allows you to feature multiple voices from your business as hosts and co-hosts and lets you bring in guests for interviews. You get the prestige of having a radio show on a "known" radio station, which helps to gain credibility with your audience. While there will be a lot of pressure to have the hosts be professional, engaging, and entertaining, a show that keeps listeners tuned in will highlight you as a personality in the real estate business. For examples check out www.mnrealestateshow.com and www.mnhometalk.com these are just two of the handful of agent teams that have AM Radio shows here in Minnesota.

PODCASTING

All of that said, for a smaller investment, you can achieve many of the same goals as a well-produced podcast. You can quickly experiment with your own podcast with equipment and applications that you probably already have on your phone or home computer. If you decide to get serious about podcasting, Matt Johnson with pursuingresults.com is a great resource.

If you find that you have a knack for podcasting, you can promote it via your social media, your website, and via guest appearances on the podcasts of other real estate agents. For a nominal investment, you could also hire a PR or marketing firm to help you better produce or promote your podcast such as Vryal Marketing (www.getvyral.com)

By taking some of the principles of radio advertising and applying them to podcasting, you'll be ahead of the game when it comes to promoting your services and reaching audiences far and wide.

RESOURCES

www.radioandtelevisionexperts.com

www.pursuingresults.com

www.getvyral.com

BILLBOARDS

Kris Lindahl is hands down the king of bill-boards, you can't drive down any major freeway in Minnesota without seeing one of them. He had also managed to leverage the exposure from all of his billboards into additional PR when the Vikings played the Eagles in Philadelphia for a shot to play in the super bowl here which was held here in Minnesota. He had the balls to put up a big purple & yellow billboard right outside of the Eagle's stadium and even show up for the game. The Vikings didn't win, but he did receive a tremendous amount of support from fans back home. Later on, he donated space on a billboard he paid for to bring back a Michael Jordan inspired photo of WNBA Lynx player Maya Moore, which generated more positive publicity. Now I'm not saying you need 30+ billboards like Kris has to be effective, but it isn't realistic to think that you can buy just one billboard and expect to see results. In fact, it can be quite difficult to get your message across when cars are whizzing by at 70+ mph and likely staring at their phone. Yikes! However, the numbers are there to prove that billboards can drive awareness of a brand, but only when advertised correctly. Over 54% will recognize an image or logo, but less than 20% will recall a website or phone number that they see on the billboard. Less than 1% will remember any text from the billboard.

THE COSTS OF BILLBOARD CAMPAIGNS

Billboards are costly to produce and fall into the same price range as TV commercials.

According to FitSmallBusiness.com, many different aspects can affect how much you will pay for billboard advertising. Three primary factors are:

Circulation: The total volume of traffic that passes the billboard, which is derived from transportation authorities. The amount of circulation does not take into account whether passersby see your ad or not.

Demographics: The breakdown by age, gender and income level of people who typically pass by a billboard. Expect to pay more to advertise to people with higher income levels.

Impressions: The number of people who see the ad, based on the size of the billboard, visibility, the average speed at which people are passing, etc. This information is derived from the circulation and the geo-positioning of the billboard.

Together, these factors make up the Out-of-Home (OOH) ratings of a billboard, which is the standard set of measurements used by ad agencies. For more on these ratings, you can check out Geopath, the premier out of home ("OOH") advertising ratings organization.

Similar to TV advertising markets, you will pay more for prime spots. For example, billboards in downtown New York will be significantly higher than a billboard in a rural area.

In addition to the location and length of time costs, there are costs for production. To begin with, you will need someone to design the billboard, if you do not have the time or the expertise to do it yourself. Freelancers can run from $500 to $1,000. An agency will be a bit higher: $5,000 to $10,000. You can go beyond just traditional billboards and stand out with more 3D designs (e.g., the Chik-Fil-A Cows) but plan on that as an added cost.

Vinyl is the standard material used for the ad itself because of its resistance to weather. The cost of printing an advertisement on vinyl for a bulletin billboard (14' by 48', or almost 700 square feet of material) runs between $300-$500.

You would typically think that digital billboards would be cheaper to acquire. Yes, it is cheaper to produce the actual billboard, as it is a high-resolution digital image, but there is a catch. Because the billboard companies have wised up and converted some of their highest trafficked locations to digital, you are stuck paying for those more premiere sites. A digital campaign will add about 10 to 20% more than a traditional billboard.

However, for your real estate business, a digital billboard provides a unique opportunity: you will have the ability to easily and quickly update the information on your ad to promote new listings or to update your photo. Additional costs may be incurred to update the image, but it is far more efficient than planning a whole new print campaign

According to thebalance.com, a leading financial interest website, here are some best practices for any billboard campaign:

- Six Words or Less is Ideal. Considering we're on the move when we read billboards, we don't have a lot of time to take them in. Six seconds is the accepted industry average for reading a billboard. So, around six words are all you should use to get your message across. Concision is tough, but headlines that are small paragraphs will not get read. If you have a sophisticated brand, product or service, you should stay away from billboards completely.

- Get Noticed, But Don't Be a Huge Distraction. Most of the time, billboards target drivers, bikers, cyclists or pedestrians. You have just a few seconds to get a message across to people who are on the move, which causes an interesting dilemma for the advertiser; you want to get noticed, but you don't want to be responsible for any accidents.

- Billboards are not for Direct Response. There are some genuinely awful billboards covered in phone numbers and website addresses. And without a doubt, people are not calling that number or visiting that website.

- Billboards are an effective secondary advertising medium, which means that it's ideal for brand-building and supporting a campaign, but it just cannot do the heavy lifting. Billboards are the wrong medium for anything other than a quick message.

- Be Smart, But Not Too Smart. A boring billboard will get no attention. A smart billboard will grab the attention and leave a lasting impression. A billboard that's trying too hard to be clever, well, more than likely, it will get lost on the audience.

- The More Billboards, The Better. One billboard is not cheap. But it's also not very practical either. Billboards are a mass market medium, but they need more than one location. You want as many eyes on them as possible, which by itself is a compelling argument to go with digital billboards to get on more signs in heavily trafficked areas.

- Show It, don't say it. Get creative with your billboard ideas. A flat billboard is the standard, but it doesn't have to be the norm.

- Keep It Simple, Stupid. A billboard is a quick read. Most of the time, you see it as you speed past it in your car, so it needs to get the message across as efficiently as possible.

- Be Wary of Logo Size. You may be tempted to spend your valuable space on your logo. That would ring true if your logo were easily recognizable like the Golden Arches or the Coca-Cola ribbon. If your log is not that iconic, it is better to match logo with words that make an impact and drives awareness.

While it is difficult to quantify the number of leads a billboard campaign gets you, they are undoubtedly an advanced and powerful option when your business is ready, and when your advertising budget allows it.

RESOURCES

www.outfrontmedia.com

www.clearchanneloutdoor.com

VEHICLE WRAP

A vehicle wrap is a very large vinyl decal applied directly to the original paint of a car or truck. Sometimes called Vehicle Graphics, they can wrap around the entirety of the vehicle, or just be applied to windows, doors, or panels. You've undoubtedly seen some of these, advertising everything from pizza to healthcare, and varying in terms of effectiveness.

Vehicle wrap companies make it easy to create an original design to your specifications that will fit your car. Like most other things, with wraps, the consensus is that you get what you pay for, so this is one thing you don't want to cheap out on if you decide to go that route.

Taste-wise, vehicle wraps are as varied as can be imagined. In any case, vehicle wraps advertising your real estate business will surely make a statement. Before you plunk down anywhere from a couple of hundred dollars for customized magnets for your car, to upwards of $2k for a full vehicle wrap, here are some pros and cons of vehicle wraps.

PRO

- Most vehicle wraps can be done in one day, meaning minimal downtime for you

- The average lifespan of a vehicle wrap is around 3-5 years, meaning that, thanks to the lack of a monthly payment, your ad could recoup your investment many times over in that period, even in light of the high cost of a full-body wrap

- If your ad is unusual (but still in good taste), people may take photos and post it to their social media, thereby doing a great deal of additional advertising for you at no additional cost

- People like to work with people who are like them; when you drive your car to partake in your favorite hobby, like paintball, you have already passed a kind of test with your fellow enthusiasts, making them trust you more and keeping you top of mind when they need or know someone who needs an agent

- There's no risk of having to share advertising space with other agents, or to bid for prime placement, as is the case in print publications or billboards

- If you frequently drive, being seen around town all the time heightens impact and the number of impressions; all in all, vehicle wraps are a very cost-effective method of advertising when compared to things like billboards, radio and TV ads, and printed advertisements

CONS

- Your business will be under scrutiny as you drive around, so you must be an incredibly courteous driver at all times. Don't do things that would cause others to get a negative impression of you as you drive around advertising your company. I may have gotten a call or two about my impeccable driving.

- If you plan on wrapping a leased car, you may need to check first to see if a vehicle wrap voids any terms of your contract.

- There's no way to track how effective your wrapped vehicle is in getting you leads, but you will hear people say "I see you everywhere."

- The lifespan of a wrap is affected by many variables, including the skill of the technician applying it, and weather. Also, keeping your wrap looking fresh throughout its lifespan requires maintenance, as things like fingerprints and oil stains need special attention to remove

- When it comes time to remove your wrap, you may need to get professional assistance to avoid causing damage to your car's original paint and body.

A reputable wrap company will be happy to work with you to design your wrap. While vehicle wraps might still be considered outside-the-box thinking currently, this is one case where it might pay not to follow the crowd. I've wrapped 3 vehicles so far and will continue to do so as long as I'm a business owner.

NEW CONSTRUCTION

As the housing market continues to recover from the 2008 economic crisis, new construction is booming. Recent reports indicate that construction spending soared across all sectors of the real estate industry in 2017. Depending on your market and selling style, new development can be a fulfilling and lucrative niche for you.

WORKING WITH BUYERS

Regarding new construction, there's a common misconception among buyers that the process is simple and straightforward: they just walk into the builder's office, pick their lot and design, and then sign, right? Many have no idea that the person they're speaking to is working on behalf of the builder and doesn't have their best interest in mind. This is where you come in.

Attend open houses in the new development or sponsor strategically placed ads to let buyers know that you can provide essential services like helping to find a reputable builder, going to bat for them to review contracts, assisting with negotiations, and helping them choose smart upgrade choices. Stay up to date on the inventory available, popular trends and let buyers know which upgrades provide best resale value.

On our website, we post information about all of the new developments including available lots, pricing, styles of homes, and nearby amenities. Builders don't always list all of their pricing or plans on MLS so it's important to know what is available for buyers that they may not already be aware of. By writing about the different communities, you're demonstrating your local expertise and will generate some organic website traffic from potential buyers search for new construction online.

Some agents have success offering a discount or rebate on the sale of new homes, often times this can be tied to listing their current home. This way you'll end up with two sales in one, often times the commission paid by the builder will be greater than the list side commission from selling their back up home.

As with other forms of marketing, keep track of the ROI you're getting from this kind of advertising; you might just find a niche for yourself in new construction and can allocate more of your advertising budget.

When you're working with clients who are building, take pictures of the property as progress has been made. You can put all of the pictures together in a photobook from Shutterfly or Snapfish online and present it to them as a gift at closing.

WORKING WITH BUILDERS AND DEVELOPERS

Realtors and home builders have a unique relationship; they need one another, but, as is the case with many long-term relationships, there must be an open channel of communication, the right attitudes, and a whole lot of work.

Builders who want to be successful know that the realtor community is a valuable resource for not only pre-sale clients but to help with sales presentations and open houses. While these relationships can be tenuous due to the high stakes involved, it doesn't have to be that way. Take the time to carefully choose a builder to make new construction a viable option for your business.

You can either work with the builder directly or the builder's representative. What's most important is to set realistic expectations of your relationship with the builder and get on the same page as quickly as possible, or you may find yourself in a time-consuming relationship that takes far more than it gives.

National builders typically employ full-time representatives who are not allowed to represent other clients. While they are W-2 employees with benefits such as 401k and health insurance they do have set hours including weekends. The builder typically handles all of the marketing and has a set of options. Representatives are responsible for knowing and selling the product, there is an art to building the experience.

Working with builders or developers may take up a majority of your time; if you fail to get your terms out in the open right away, you might miss out on valuable, more profitable opportunities elsewhere that will make you regret starting a relationship with the builder in the first place.

You can find builders and developers to work with by contacting trade groups and builders associations. Do your homework on each candidate to find a reputable partner with extensive knowledge of their market. Lastly, the quality of construction between different builders may vary wildly, so be sure to do your research there as well so that you don't get stuck trying to sell properties below your standards, or whose association will cast you or your business in a less than favorable light.

RESOURCES

Builders associations
Open Houses

VIDEO MARKETING

Video marketing is a fast-growing marketing tactic for professionals in all industries. However, for one reason or another, real estate agents and brokers have not been so quick to implement the power of video marketing for their businesses, to their detriment.

For those agents that do use videos in their marketing, most use videos to show off a listing or a property. While this is good practice to build and strengthen your staging, visual and scripting skills, these kinds of videos aren't useful for much beyond that, mainly because once the house sells, the videos are of no use. You might be able to provide some value with this kind of videos for your fellow agents, or for your protégés by using your best (or worst) ones as teaching tools and examples.

If you're nervous about making a video, it's easy to get started and experiment without too much investment in time or equipment. If you carry a smartphone, you have everything you need. Some tips to keep in mind are:

- Avoid backlighting: make sure we can see you, or whatever you want to show us. If the light source, be it the sun or even just a desk lamp, is behind the object, we won't be able to see it and will lose interest.

- Make a script: even if it's just a few bullet points on an index card, have a plan for what you want to say. Nothing extinguishes interest like rambling delivery.

- Keep trying: shoot your first video, and experiment with editing. By the time you've gotten a few under your belt, you'll have a good idea of how you want to come across, and what you may want to do differently.

When you get to the point where you are ready to share your videos on your website or social media, you might decide that you need more sophisticated quality; you can invest in better equipment or hire a video marketing service to help you create videos you can be proud of.

Now that you know some basics of how to get started in video marketing, here are some smart uses of video marketing for your real estate business:

- Community videos: sell the lifestyle of your market. Create videos about your market or community that showcase amenities like parks, theatres, recreational activities, popular restaurants, revitalized neighborhoods, etc. Whatever makes your community a desirable place to live, go out and film it.

- Video testimonials: ask past clients whom you think had a positive experience with you if they'd be willing to sit for a video testimonial for your business. You would post your video to your website, social media accounts, or include it in an email message (more on that below). However, a word of caution: don't merely ask your former clients to come in and sit against a blank wall and talk about how great you are. Have a staging area ready and have specific questions to ask, such as "what led you to sell your home in the first place?", and "What did I do best to help you find or sell your home?"

- Agent Profiles: Chances are, you're more comfortable speaking to clients and leads in person than in text. Videos on your website are a great chance to introduce yourself on your terms; letting potential clients get a sense of who you are, how you work, and what sets you apart from other agents.

- Company Profiles: Like agent profiles, videos that profile your team or company are a great way to show what's unique about your service. You can tell the story of your company, highlight notable successes, and create a personal connection to get viewers engaged.

The growing trend for video marketing is to incorporate it into things like email – a leading resource is a company called BombBomb, which, at the time of this writing, is a cutting-edge resource for video email, customized for real estate agents.

Like any innovative tool, BombBomb is continuously evolving so we won't go into too much detail about what they offer your real estate business. Suffice to say that they are a vital tool for standing out in the email inboxes of your contact list. Bombbomb makes it easy to create professional-looking videos with tools that tell you what's working, and can be used for individualized contact with clients, or to launch a full-blown marketing campaign.

Generally speaking the best use of your video marketing time and money is to build connections, relationships and to share information, as opposed to getting leads or sales. Quality video marketing may well garner you more leads and referrals than you ever imagined, but as the most effective videos focus on creating and strengthening the human connection, focusing on being genuine will go much further than using them to show off what you have to sell.

RESOURCES

YouTube

Vimeo

BombBomb

PUTTING IT ALL TOGETHER

While the industry may be veering more and more toward all things digital, there's still something to be said for the power of tried and true traditional marketing. Imagine combining the best of both worlds: the reach and ingenuity of digital marketing, with the proven effectiveness of conventional methods. After all, an effectively delivered, well-crafted message is at the heart of a successful marketing campaign, and this end can be accomplished both online and in-person. Take a look at the breakdown below to learn the sharpest ways to intersect traditional and digital marketing campaigns.

THINK *ENHANCEMENT,* NOT *REPLACEMENT*

Instead of putting all your eggs in one basket, it's wise to merge digital and traditional marketing methods to get the most out of both. For instance, a simple skim through a print magazine proves that physical ads are still an effective method of promoting a business's social media identity. Likewise, a social media post might highlight an upcoming feature in a print publication.

Let's dig deeper - perhaps the contacts and leads you've cultivated online can be targeted through personalized print mailers. By blending the digital and traditional, you've taken an online connection and created an opportunity in the physical world.

Passive vs. Active Campaigns

Traditional marketing methods can disseminate a message and help shape brand identity, but these are considered passive approaches. Even mailers, commercials, and radio spots that have a call to action woven in aren't quite interactive in the way that digital marketing can be. However, despite the failings of traditional passive marketing, the truth remains that it casts a wide net and reaches a broad audience—an invaluable tool when cultivating business or establishing your presence in a new area.

Meanwhile, active digital campaigns—across social media or through e-mail blasts—can hone in on a specific audience with a particular need. Click-through options, contact forms, shareable social media, and the like create an active opportunity for your potential clientele.

CULTIVATING A GRAND PRESENCE AND A PERSONAL CONNECTION

Consider a real estate agent with attractive signage who showcases on the lawns of all the properties he or she represents - they generate awareness and authority in the area, but they aren't necessarily *con*necting with potential clients or identifying themselves as a professional. You can elevate this traditional approach by promoting social media channels on the signage, where an agent can better express his or her voice, working style, areas of expertise, and even relatable personal tastes.

Traditional methods like signage, billboards, mailers, and print ads play an integral role in your company's professional image, but digital marketing can take that presence many steps further—transforming a business into a personalized service with a distinct voice.

All in all, traditional and digital marketing aren't at odds with one another. Ideally, both work in a complementary fashion, upping your efforts, presence, and impact by bridging the gap between two essential marketplaces. Keep these ideas and examples in mind as you merge the best of traditional and digital marketing to give your business a decisive boost.

THE IMPORTANCE OF TRACKING AND MEASURING ROI

Tracking and measuring your return on investment, or ROI allows you an in-depth, data-backed picture of where your marketing dollars are going, and how they perform. No one wants to pour resources into a campaign that yields no fruitful results. That's why taking stock of your marketing efforts, down to the number, helps you determine the best use of your time and funds for maximum effectiveness. Below, you'll find a few concrete reasons why measuring and tracking ROI should be a foundational tenet of your marketing routine, and how adopting this habit can meaningfully impact your business.

TRACKING YOUR ROI SEPARATES THE IDEAL FROM THE MEDIOCRE.

While the instinct may be to cover all your bases when it comes to traditional and digital marketing, isn't it wiser to choose the medium that's yielded concrete returns? Tracking the effectiveness of your ROI creates a clear correlation between your marketing expenditures and how many leads and clients you've reaped as a result. Even just engaging with new clients about where they found your services can give you a good picture. If almost all of them found you online, you know that investing in your digital presence is a better choice than continuing running print ads. Casting a wide net isn't always a bad thing, but the more efficient and cost-effective option is to double down on what you know is working. By tracking and measuring your ROI, you have the hard data to make the correct allocation choices.

Measuring ROI determines how much each new client costs.

Data measuring can be liberating because it takes abstract concepts and distills them into evidence-based information. If you take the time to track and measure ROI, you'll know exactly how much you spent on marketing last year and how many new clients you earned as a result. This information helps you determine how many marketing dollars you're spending per new client, which is useful on many fronts. To name just a few, you can decide whether you're spending too much or too little on marketing, which marketing channel is most cost-effective for reeling in new leads, and how much profit you're making on a per-client basis.

Tracking and Measuring ROI works as your own personal fortune teller.

While you can't account for every foreseeable future scenario, tracking and measuring your ROI is an excellent way to get a glimpse down the road. If you have weeks, months, or years or data that show personalized marketing trends, you can make informed decisions based on what's already transpired. Marketing doesn't have to be a best-guess game. Instead, you can use tailor-made data to make informed decisions, time and again, or learn from missteps and avoid making them in the future. This empowers you to waste fewer dollars on unsuccessful outlets and reduce your stress along the way.

Instead of gambling your marketing budget, treat your business like the well-oiled machine it deserves to be. Invest the time in gathering ROI data, and you'll be able to make smarter decisions based on a verifiable track record. Doing so allows your business to grow, become more efficient and productive, and allows you to forecast your professional future.

If this book has been successful, you now have a number of ideas to help you stand out from the competition. You know to be patient with each tactic that you try, to measure your results, and to be patient when gathering data.

Most importantly, you have a better idea of the kinds of tactics that might work for you, and you know that it is not humanly possible to attempt every marketing idea in this book.

Did I miss anything? Let me know, I'd love to hear from you!
brandon@bdoyleconsulting.com

This playbook wouldn't be possible if it weren't for the contribution of fellow agents who have shared their experiences on stage, online and in person. The way we market ourselves changes every day as the industry evolves, and we can all learn from each other. If you feel you're the expert on a particular topic or have a great story to tell, let me know, and we can collaborate on future editions. In the meantime, please share with colleagues in industry and leave an honest review on Amazon.

RESOURCES

Sphere of Influence follow up & email marketing

http://www.contactually.com
http://www.first.io
http://www.limelightmarketingsystems.com
http://www.mailchimp.com
http://www.happygrasshopper.com

Networking Events

www.Eventbrite.com
www.Meetup.com
https://www.bni.com/
https://www.networkafterwork.com/

Referral Networks

www.referralexchange.com
www.homelight.com
www.agentpronto.com

ONLINE PRESENCE

Business.google.com
Facebook.com/pages
Moz.com/local
Yext
BrightLocal
Yelp.com

WEBSITES

Domains - GoDaddy.com
Broke Websites - TRIBUS
Team Websites - Firepoint.net Boomtownroi.com
Commissionsinc.com
Full Custom Team/Individual Websites - Cuyrator,
Real Estate Webmasters
Individual Template Websites - Chime, Agent Image,
TorchX

3RD PARTY PORTALS

www.zillow.com
www.realtor.com
www.homes.com
www.callaction.co

FACEBOOK ADVERTISING

Homesnap.com
BackatYouMedia.com
AdRoll.com
Business.facebook.com

Social Tools

www.facebook.com
www.linkedin.com
www.twitter.com
www.instagram.com
www.Hootsuite.com
www.HubSpot.com
www.Tweetdeck.com
www.Buffer.com
www.SproutSocial.com

Open House Tools

Open House Pro
Realtors Property Resource®
Homesnap

Probate Leads

www.AllTheLeads.com
www.SuccessorsData.com

Expired Tools

Arch Agent
Landvoice
Mojo Dialer
RedX

FSBO SOURCES

Zillow Make Me Move
Craigslist
Nextdoor
Facebook Marketplaces

MARKET DATA

Realtors Property Resource®
Infosparks
MLS Market Data

GEOGRAPHIC FARMING

www.GeographicFarm.com
www.corefact.com
www.Remine.com
www.smartzip.com
www.Eddm.usps.com

HOME VALUATION LEADS

www.primesellerleads.com
www.Geographicfarm.com
www.Curaytor.com
www.BoldLeads.com
www.Listing2Leads.com
www.HomeValueLeads.com

SIGNS

Callaction.co
Lowen Signs
Build A Sign

RELOCATION

SIRVA
Crown World Mobility
Cartus
WorldWideERC.org

BILLBOARDS

www.outfrontmedia.com
www.clearchanneloutdoor.com

RADIO & PODCASTS

www.radioandtelevisionexperts.com
www.pursuingresults.com
www.getvyral.com

BOOK RECOMMENDATIONS

Ninja Selling: Subtle Skills. Big Results. by Larry Kendall

The Conversion Code: Capture Internet Leads, Create Quality Appointments, Close More Sales by Chris Smith

The 4-Hour Workweek: Escape 9-5, Live Anywhere, and Join the New Rich by Timothy Ferris

Mindset, Methods & Metrics: Winning as a Modern Real Estate Agent by Brandon Doyle, Nicholas Dreher & Marshall Saunders

The Million Dollar Real Estate Team: How I went from Zero to Earning $1 Million after Expenses in Three Years by Christopher Watters

How to be a Great Salesperson by Monday Morning by David Cook

Listing Boss: The Definitive Blueprint for Real Estate Success by Hoss Pratt

Secrets of Top Selling Agents: The Keys To Real Estate Success Revealed by Joe Sesso

Explosive Sales Growth in Real Estate by Ryan Snow

Mindset, Model & Marketing!: The Proven Strategies to Transform and Grow Your Real Estate Business by Tom Ferry

Profit First by Mike Michalowicz

Content Machine by Dan Norris

Harris Rules by Tim & Julie Harris

REAL A path to Passion, Purpose, and Profits in Real Estate by Dave Crumby, Lani Rosales, and Martin Streicher

Disruptors, Discounters, and Doubters by Joe Rand

The Miracle Morning by Hal Elrod

Shift How Top Real Estate Agents Tackle Tough Times by Gary Keller with Dave Jenks and Jay Papasan

The Millionaire Real Estate Agent by Gary Keller with Dave Jenks and Jay Papasan

The ONE Thing: The Surprisingly Simple Truth Behind Extraordinary Results by Gary Keller and Jay Papasan

#GetSocialSmart by Katie Lance

The Politically Incorrect Real Estate Agent Handbook (and companion Log-book) by Peter F. Porgelli Jr.

Billion Dollar Agent Manifesto: Secrets to Grow Your Business to Over $1,000,000 by Best Agent Business (Steve Kantor)

7L: The Seven Levels of Communication: Go from Relationships to Referrals by Michael J. Maher

The 7 Habits of Highly Effective People: Powerful Lessons in Personal Change by Stephen R. Covey

Outrageous Authenticity: You Are Your Best Sales Weapon by Leigh Brown

The Go-Giver by Bob Burg, John David Mann

Growth Hacker Marketing by Ryan Holiday

Purple Cow: Transform Your Business by Being Remarkable by Seth Godin

The Compound Effect: Jumpstart Your Income, Your Life, Your Success by Darren Hardy

The Thank You Economy by Gary Vaynerchuck

Drive: The Surprising Truth About What Motivates Us by Daniel H. Pink

Blue Ocean Strategy: How to Create Uncontested Market Space and Make Competition Irrelevant by Grover Gardner

Start with Why: How Great Leaders Inspire Everyone to Take Action by Simon Sinek

Everybody Lies: Big Data, New Data and What the Internet Can Tell Us About Who We Really Are by Seth Stephens-Davidowitz

Never Split The Difference: Negotiating as if Your Life Depended on it by Chris Voss

Fanatical Prospecting: The Ultimate Guide for Starting Sales Conversations and Filling the Pipeline by Leveraging Social Selling, Telephone, E-Mail, and Cold Calling by Jeb Blount

The Tipping Point: How Little Things Can Make a Big Difference by Malcolm Gladwell

Think and Grow Rich by Napoleon Hill

Good to Great by Jim Collins

Hacking Growth: How Today's Fastest-Growing Companies Drive Breakout Success by Morgan Brown and Sean Ellis

Influence: The Psychology of Persuasion by Robert B. Cialdini

High-Performance Habits: How Extraordinary People Become That Way by Brendon Burchard

The Book of YES: The Ultimate Real Estate Agent Conversion Guide by Kevin Ward

Your 1st Year in Real Estate by Dirk Zeller

Winning Real Estate: 9 Secrets to Success from Leading Pros by Century 21 Real Estate LLC

The Road To Recognition: The A-to-Z Guide to Personal Branding for Accelerating Your Professional Success in the Age of Digital Media by Seth Price & Barry Feldman

E-Myth Revisited by Michael E. Gerber

The Power of Habit: Why We Do What We Do in Life and Business by Charles Duhigg

48 Laws of Power by Robert Greene

The Five Dysfunctions of a Team: A Leadership Fable by Patrick Lencioni

Made in the USA
Coppell, TX
16 February 2020

15868269R00098